The Rhode Island Gardener's Companion

Gardener's Companion Series

The Rhode Island Gardener's Companion

An Insider's Guide to Gardening in the Ocean State

Barbara Gee

Happy gardening!
Barbara Gee

gpp

Guilford, Connecticut

The information in this book has been carefully researched. The author and publisher assume no responsibility for accidents happening to, injuries sustained, or any damage, loss, or inconvenience incurred by the reader as a result of following the information in this book. When using any commercial product, always read and follow label directions. Mention of a trade name does not imply endorsement by the publisher.

To buy books in quantity for corporate use or incentives, call **(800) 962–0973** or e-mail **premiums@GlobePequot.com.**

Text design by Casey Shain
Illustrations by Josh Yunger
Map by M.A. Dubé © Morris Book Publishing, LLC

Library of Congress Cataloging-in-Publication Data

Gee, Barbara.
  The Rhode Island gardener's companion : an insider's guide to gardening in the Ocean State / Barbara Gee.
      p. cm. — (Gardener's companion series)
  Includes index.
  ISBN-13: 978-0-7627-4485-5
  1. Gardening—Rhode Island. I. Title.
  SB453.2.R4G44 2008
  635.09745—dc22

                                                    2007042833

Manufactured in the United States of America
First Edition/First Printing

*To Julie Morris and Ginny Purviance, my friends and mentors,
and to Jeffrey, Samara, and Danya always*

Contents

Introduction

The smallest of the fifty states, it's the unique size of Rhode Island that I find so appealing. That and its incredible beauty and wide variety of landscapes. Those of us who live here will find ourselves gardening on a salt marsh, a freshwater lagoon, a mountain (well, sort of), a beach, a river, a granite ledge, a kettle hole, a glacial lake, a bay, or an island—each geological feature within miles of each other. With only 1,200 square miles to work with, the State of Rhode Island and Providence Plantations (the state's official name) has more than 400 miles of coastline. That's a lot of seaside gardening!

Gardening challenges abound in the Ocean State, including acidic soil, low fertility, sand, salt, wind, rock, and coal deposits, but that's never stopped Rhode Island gardeners. After all, the official state motto is Hope, and Little Rhody has many great resources that provide hope as well as garden wisdom, including Blithewold Mansion, Gardens & Arboretum in Bristol, one of only two arboreta in the country situated on salt water, and Providence's Roger Williams Park Botanical Center, which opened in 2007. The latter has outdoor gardens as well as the largest indoor public display gardens in New England. Adding to this bounty, the state proudly boasts one of the country's most active master gardener programs, at the University of Rhode Island.

From my years writing about gardening in New England, and as a state editor for the Northeast garden magazine *People, Places & Plants*, I have gained a deep appreciation of the topographic and climate differences in Rhode Island. Originally a city girl from London, I have a soft spot for city gardens, like those in Providence and Newport, but I have discovered and fallen in love with seaside gardens like the ones you find on Jamestown or Block Island.

This book addresses the specific challenges of gardening in

Rhode Island—the state's soil, climate, hardiness zones, growing conditions, challenges, and special places. You will find great plant recommendations from Rhode Island gardeners, proven tips for helping your plants thrive, and a chapter of state-specific resources from which you can gather yet more information to make your gardening endeavors a success. A glossary and an index round out the book.

I came to gardening a little later in life, when I moved from a city condominium in Brookline in greater Boston to a house on Aquidneck Island, so I learned to garden fast. I enrolled in the Cooperative Extension Master Gardener program at URI and then continued my studies with the Royal Horticultural Society's course for certification in horticulture. I worked at Conway's Nursery for Uncommon Plants in Tiverton, with Middletown landscape gardener Virginia Purviance, and with Julie Morris and the staff in the department of horticulture at Blithewold. And as a writer I get to meet and learn from some of the best gardeners in the state. Many of these generous folks have shared their knowledge of Rhode Island gardening to make *The Rhode Island Gardener's Companion* a really useful resource. Space constraints prevent me from thanking them all by name, but you will find them quoted throughout the book, and to each one I extend my gratitude.

I hope this book provides you with recommendations and resources that will be useful wherever you garden in the Ocean State. Write to me with your suggestions and comments care of The Globe Pequot Press, P.O. Box 480, Guilford, CT 06437-0480.

Firm
Foundations

Soils

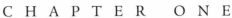

How many of us think about—and I mean *really think about*—our soil? We're often so busy "gardening" that the only indication we have of soil problems is when plants don't grow. Then too often we figure it's too little water, disease, lack of attention—anything but the soil. In fact, *poor soil contributes to 80 percent of plant growing problems.*

Good soil is *alive,* positively pulsating with life and rich in microbes, insects, nutrients, moisture, and oxygen. Poor soil, on the other hand, is dull, pale, colorless—literally lifeless. A scarcity of worms is a pretty good indication that the soil is dead.

Getting to know your soil and what it needs is key. Quite simply, good soil is the foundation of a good garden. To get the most out of yours, let's take a moment to look at the big picture: why we have the soil we have in Rhode Island, where it came from, how it was formed, and if it is good or bad.

What Is Soil?

Soil begins with the breakdown of rocks into small mineral particles by environmental factors: wind, rain, heat, and cold. Factor in the accumulation of decaying organic materials such as leaves and grass; the chemistry that happens when roots move through the soil; the activity of organisms such as microbes, insects, earthworms, and humans attacking organic matter; the topography of the land; and time. The end result is soil.

Good soil is essential to plant health. It supports plants, holding them in place. It is a source of the nutrients, moisture, and air (oxygen) they need. Good soil is a balance of the correct proportions of minerals, nutrients, air, water, and beneficial insects and animals. It holds enough water for plant needs yet drains well enough that the plants and animal life don't suffocate. We're not all blessed with good soil on our property—but we can create it.

A well-balanced surface soil is made up of approximately half solid material and half open spaces. Some of the soil particles are big enough to see easily, while others are so small you'd need a microscope to view them. Most soils are classified based on the amount of sand, clay, or silt they contain and are usually a combination of these mineral elements in different amounts.

- Sand or gravel particles are the largest. They don't hold water well but let air into the soil.

- Clay particles are very small and can compact, which means that water does not drain through efficiently and air can't get in easily.

- Silt particles are medium size, in between sand and clay.

Sandy soils are found through most of the state and are particularly noticeable in the western part of the Narragansett Basin, which includes Providence, Cranston, Warwick, and North Kingston. Sandy soils have low levels of nutrients and lose nutrients fairly fast due to fast drainage. These soils have less clay in them and therefore hold less water. Sandy soils usually have low levels of organic matter, but any organic matter that is added will break down quickly and improve the texture. Sandy soil warms up quickly in the spring and is easy to work when wet. When dry it can be dusty and difficult to handle.

Clay soils are rarely found in Rhode Island except for small pockets like Aquidneck Island, Little Compton, and Block Island. Clay soils are heavy to work and slow to drain but can be very fertile. These soils hold water too well and become waterlogged and compacted, which makes it difficult for plants to get access to either air or water. They are slow to warm up in the spring. Clay soils shouldn't be worked when wet because they can be easily damaged. When dry they tend to shrink. One advantage of clay soil is that it holds high levels of nutrients; however, the nutrients aren't easily available to the plants. Clay soil requires good management to make the nutrients available.

Silty soils are found in South County and around Newport. They are fairly easy to work when dry, but like sandy soils they can be dry and dusty. Water is easily absorbed into these soils but can contribute to erosion. They are less easy to work when wet and tend to compact easily. Silty soils are slow to warm up in spring. They have only moderate levels of organic matter and nutrients.

Few soils are all sand or all silt. Most soils are a mix: gravelly sand, loamy sand, stony sandy loam, silt loam, silty clay loam, clay loam, sandy clay, sandy clay loam—and so on.

Soils in Rhode Island

Rhode Island's topography was formed in the most recent ice age. Twenty-two thousand years ago the whole state was covered with a mile-thick glacier. About 17,000 years ago the ice started to retreat. Narragansett Bay and Rhode Island Sound were dry lakebeds until approximately 12,000 years ago, when sea levels began to rise.

As the glacier ice moved through the area, it rearranged the land like a bulldozer, crunching up rock and depositing material, known as glacial deposits, in its wake. As the ice melted it carried materials (known as glacial outwash) away from the northern hills toward the ocean. Glacial outwash is found all over Rhode Island, notably in Squantum Woods State Park in East Providence, where large boulders of sandstone and granite may well have been transported from more than 20 miles away. And Block

Island did not exist prior to the ice age.

Chunks of ice detached from the retreating glacier and, once the ice melted, formed depressions known as kettle holes. These can be seen today in areas like South County. If the water didn't drain, the kettle holes became ponds, such as Toupoyesett Pond. If larger than a pond, they are officially called glacial lakes, like Watchaug Pond in the Kimball Wildlife Refuge or Worden Pond in South Kingstown.

The glaciers ground up the acidic, granitic underlying bedrock into soils high in silica and quartz content—in other words, sand. "Our Rhode Island soils have less than 15 percent clay," states James Turenne, assistant Rhode Island state soil scientist. "They generally have a high sand content, which also means that overall they have fairly low fertility." Yes, there *are* areas of good fertility in the state, but according to Turenne it was the low fertility of the soil and the amount of rock fragments that drove our forebears farther west in their quest for land that was easier to farm.

In general Rhode Island soils are 65 percent glacial till, which consists mostly of sand, gravel, clay, silt, and boulders, resulting in medium to coarse texture. The remainder of Rhode Island soil is a mix of clay and silt. Sandy loams are typical of glacial till.

Two aspects of glacial till soils are problematic for the gardener: First, they tend to be quite stony. If you have large, angular boulders on your property, you are in a till soil. Second, they often have a compacted layer 2 to 4 feet below the surface. This hardpan layer restricts the downward movement of water, resulting in moderate to poor drainage, particularly in spring.

On top of the glacial deposits lies a cap of windblown fine deposits created by the action of thousands of years of hurricane-force winds. This is what Rhode Islanders garden in and on.

A quick survey of experienced Ocean State gardeners reveals many soil differences around the state. Carol Salzillo in Narragansett gardens in silty loam, Chuck DiTucci in Middletown has an "excellent loamy soil," and Dorothy Read's garden in

Kingston has sandy loam. Lori Ouimette in Warwick works with part clay, part sand; Daune Peckham in Little Compton tackles "heavy clay soil with poor drainage," and Layanee DeMerchant in Foster struggles with rocks and clay. "Beyond dead" is how Carol Fayas describes the soil she discovered in her Providence garden. Sybil Parker, however, in Matunuck states that she has "fabulous soil—the perfect loam." Where I live in Portsmouth, my soil is black, shaley, and sticky—a constant reminder that there were coal mines in the area.

What about *your* particular soil? You can discover more about what you have by examining soil surveys gathered by the Natural Resources Conservation Service. Research the surveys for your area's soil at www.nrcs .usda.gov/technical/soils.html_RI_NRCS_ soils_page.

Physical Properties of Soil

All soil is composed of three layers, known as horizons. You may have seen the three layers if you've dug down deeply or looked closely at a construction site.

Topsoil is the top horizon. It is darker because it contains organic content. Most root action takes place in this layer, and that's why plants obtain most of their water and nutrients from this surface horizon.

Subsoil, the next layer down, is lighter in color and less fertile. It tends to be a yellowish-brown color. There's less root growth in this layer.

Parent material is the third layer—this is the relatively unweathered geologic material. For most places in Rhode Island, the parent material is either till or outwash, but in some areas hard bedrock is also encountered at shallow depths. Roots cannot penetrate this third layer if the parent material is a compact glacial till or hard bedrock.

No matter what its makeup, soil is described in terms of its physical properties: texture, color, and structure.

Texture: You probably won't be able to truly identify what soil texture you have without a soil test (see the soil testing section later in the chapter), but you can quickly get a rough idea by taking some soil in your hand and rubbing it between your fingers. Sandy soil will feel gritty and won't hold together; a clay soil will remind you of pottery class—sticky, heavy, and easy to mold into a ball. Silty soil has a silky, slippery feel in your hand. If you feel inclined you can conduct complicated soil-texture tests yourself using jars of water, but the most efficient way is to send soil samples off to a lab. A soil test is essential to find out the exact texture and also the accurate pH of your soil.

Color: A soil's color is an indication of how much organic material that soil contains. The darker the color the greater the organic matter content. If the soil is light, it usually indicates that the soil has lower organic matter content, either through exces-

Do You Have Good Topsoil?

Learn what the soil is like in your own garden. If your home is built on an old potato field or on overused agricultural land, the soil may have been depleted of its nutrients. In new developments contractors often remove the topsoil, leaving the home buyer with nothing but subsoil.

sive drainage or overuse, which has depleted the soil.

Structure: Soil structure, or "tilth," is the soil's physical condition. The term *tilth* comes from the old English word for cultivating soil. A soil is said to have good tilth, or to be "friable," if it has a structure that holds together when compressed and yet crumbles easily, if it absorbs water quickly, and if the water drains easily.

Soil Chemistry, Soil pH

Nutrients become available to plants when those nutrients are dissolved in the soil. The acidity of a soil determines how well nutrients dissolve and therefore become available. If your soil is either too acid or alkaline, nutrients are either completely unavailable because they are not dissolved, or they dissolve too slowly to be useful to plants.

The term *pH* means "potential hydrogen." It is a measurement of how alkaline or acid the soil is. The pH measurement range is from 1 to 14:

- The lower end is acid: 1 to 5. Lemons have a pH of 1.3 to 2.4.

- The high end is alkaline: 8 to 14. Ammonia has a pH 10.6 to 11.6.

- Neutral pH is in the middle: 6 to 7. Pure water has a pH of 7.

A soil pH somewhere in the range of 6 to 7 will cause most plant nutrients to be available to the plants. Most Rhode Island soils are acidic, with a pH somewhere between 4.5 and 5.5, although there are exceptions. Ocean State gardeners probably won't encounter alkaline soil except for small pockets. For instance, the Lime Rock Preserve in Lincoln is underlain with limestone bedrock; hence the park's name. Some lucky folks, like Chuck DiTucci of Gardens & Landscapes in Middletown, garden in soil with pH 6.4 to 6.7, considered neutral.

It's important to measure the acidity of your soil so you know when to make improvements and when to leave well enough alone. Soil pH also affects the activity of beneficial microorganisms. The work of bacteria on the decomposition of organic matter can be slowed down or stopped entirely in highly acidic soils. What you end up with is organic matter that cannot decompose. This does nothing to improve your soil and it may cause problems like poor drainage, poor aeration, or the accumulation of harmful bacteria.

pH Preferences

The pH range that you will be working with for most plants is between 4.5 and 7.0. But you have to know what your plants want before attempting to change the pH. Here are examples of plant pH preferences:

- Bentgrass—5.5 to 6.5
- Potatoes—5.0 to 6.5
- Rhubarb—6.0 to 7.0
- Sweet corn—5.5 to 7.5
- Sweet potatoes— 5.2 to 6.0
- Turnips—5.5 to 6.8

Changing Your Soil pH

If your soil is too alkaline, which is rarely the case in Rhode Island, you will want to add sulfur to lower the pH level. The sulfur is processed into sulfuric acid. If your soil is too acidic, you'll want to add lime to raise the pH level. "Most of the time we need to lime the heck out of our Rhode Island soils," says Rhode Island state soil scientist James Turenne.

Lime requirements vary with soil type. The higher the organic content of a soil, the more lime it will take to bring about a change in pH. Lime increases nitrogen availability because it speeds up the decomposition of organic matter. Adding lime does more than just raise the level of pH in your soil—it adds calcium and magnesium to the soil and helps make phosphorus more available to the plants. The addition of lime also reduces the risk of aluminum and manganese toxicity that can occur in soil with a low pH. Remember to monitor your soil to make sure you're not adding too much lime.

Here's a simple rule of thumb to raise or lower the pH of your soil: To raise the pH one unit, mix in anywhere from two to nine pounds of limestone per 100 square feet. Some common liming materials are dolomitic limestone, which is helpful where magnesium levels are low; bonemeal; ground shells; and wood ashes from your fireplace. To lower the pH one unit, add sulfur at the rate of two to five pounds per 100 square feet.

Hot Tip

Wood ashes sweeten your soil, but use them with care! My friend Leslie Saunders in Middletown, an avid gardener, always spreads the ashes from her fireplace, but she warns that you must be sure the ashes are truly cool. "I once set my garden on fire," she says, laughing. "I didn't realize there were still warm coals in the ashes!"

Testing Your Soil

Even assuming that your Rhode Island soil is acidic, you'll still want to know what range of acidity it falls within. The most accurate method of determining your soil's pH level is to get a soil test performed at a lab (see the "Soil Test Sources" sidebar). There are, however, pH meters on the market that you can stick directly into the garden or into a soil sample that you've collected. You can also buy a soil pH testing kit, which usually comes with litmus paper and a color chart. You add soil to a little water and put the litmus paper into the solution. The paper changes color and you check it against the color chart to match it up with the color of your pH level.

Soil Test Sources

Soil tests can be performed at a private lab or a state facility. A good Web site to locate a private lab is www.attra .ncat.org/attra-pub/soil-lab. Private labs are usually more expensive than going to a state facility, however. The University of Rhode Island no longer performs soil tests, although the URI Cooperative Extension Master Gardener Program has started to train volunteers to test soils around the state. For now, the best place to go for a soil test is the University of Massachusetts Extension Service in Amherst, where they offer a variety of soil and compost tests for a relatively small fee. Get details at www.umass.edu/plsoils/ soiltest or write to the Soil and Plant Tissue Testing Laboratory, West Experiment Station, 682 North Pleasant Street, University of Massachusetts, Amherst, MA 01003. You may find the UMass Amherst brochure and soil sample kits in some local garden centers. You can also download the form from the URI Cooperative Extension Master Gardener Web site, www.urimga.org.

The soil pH may vary in different pockets of your property. Don't assume that one test will give you all the information you need. Get several tests done from samples around your yard.

Sending soil off for testing is easy. Detailed instructions are provided on the form you submit with your sample, but in simple terms you take a sample of soil anywhere from 3 to 8 inches down and send the soil in with the fee. Identify it for your own reference, particularly if you send in more than one sample.

Depending on the test you request, the soil test results will reveal the soil pH, buffer pH, extractable nutrients (such as nitrogen, iron, zinc), soil texture, soluble salts, and others.

When is the correct time to do a soil test? It depends on when you want the results. You can do a soil test in early fall to get results back in time to add amendments before winter, so the amendments can then do their work over the winter. Or you can test in the spring before you start planting to make the soil ready to receive new plants.

Cultivate to Improve Tilth

Cultivating or tilling loosens soil, helps to get air in, and breaks up compacted areas and clods. But be careful—too much tilling, digging, or turning can destroy the structure of the soil. You can end up with soil that is too fine and won't support plants well, has poor drainage, or becomes easily compacted. Timing is important, too—don't cultivate when the soil is too wet or too cold.

Improving Soils

Building up your soil is exactly like building up your own health—the stronger you are the easier it is to fight off sickness and disease, the more cheerful you are, and the more receptive you are to all things in life. It's the same for soil.

Plants need seventeen elements for normal growth. Fourteen of these come from the soil: boron, calcium, chlorine, cobalt, copper, iron, nitrogen, magnesium, manganese, molybdenum, phosphorus, potassium, sulfur, and zinc. The other three are carbon, hydrogen, and oxygen: Carbon comes from carbon dioxide; hydrogen and oxygen come from the soil water. Of these, the three major elements are nitrogen (N), phosphorus (P), and potassium (K).

You will see the "N-P-K ratio" on many garden products, including fertilizers. Each element has its own growing characteristic, but the combination of the three affects the speed of growth, the size of flower blossoms, the size and amount of fruit, the shade of green, and the strength of the stem. Nitrogen, for instance, gives a plant its dark green color and increases the growth of leaves and stems. Phosphorus stimulates the early formation and strong growth of roots, and potassium increases a plant's resistance to disease. A deficiency or excess of any of these elements will cause problems. Lack of nitrogen may result in light green to yellow leaves, and lack of potassium may result in small fruit or thin skin.

The Importance of Organic Matter

Perhaps you need to improve your soil's pH level, texture, nutrient content, amount of air, or water retention. Or maybe you need to remedy a lack of beneficial organisms like earthworms or too many harmful organisms like grubs or nematodes. You can achieve almost all of these improvements simply by adding organic matter.

Organic matter is made up of decomposed plant and animal material, or humus—great stuff for the garden. Organic material stays in the soil and keeps on working to improve it year after year. Plants can make use of the nutrients released from organic materials more easily because nutrients are released at a rate and in a way the plants can efficiently absorb them.

Incorporate an amendment into the soil by digging it in or using it as topdressing or mulch—a lot depends on how deep you want to get the material. Be aware that amendments will not work their garden magic if the soil is cold. The chemistry begins when the soil temperature goes above 40 degrees.

Here's a closer look at commonly available amendments:

Animal manure is a wonderful amendment, but you have to be careful when using it. You should not use animal manure on plants you intend to eat because of the possible transference of disease pathogens. Manure must be aged. Fresh manure can be too strong and burn plants. It may also contain viable weed seeds and disease pathogens. Get your manure from a trusted source. Aged manure should not have an unpleasant odor. Manures are designated "hot" or "cold" depending on the amount of nitrogen and fluid content: Cow and pig manures are cold; horse, sheep, and hen manures are hot.

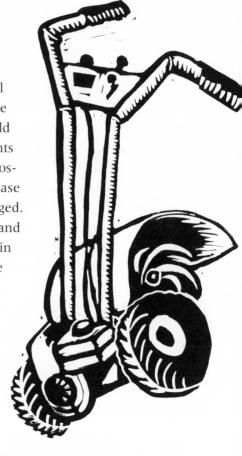

Organic slow-release fertilizers with names like Earth Juice and Cockadoodle Doo are excellent amendments. They add minerals other than just nitrogen, phosphorus, and potassium. Their N-P-K ratio will be more in the range of 5-3-3 or 4-2-3 instead of the 10-10-10 you commonly find in synthetic fertilizers. The numbers are lower, but this is not an indication of the power of these products.

Why use organic fertilizers instead of the less-expensive chemical or synthetic forms? "Synthetic fertilizers don't improve the soil," says Rich Pederson, manager of City Farm at Southside Community Land Trust in Providence. "Putting organic matter back into the soil is a much better long-term way of improving soil." And improving your soil is the goal. Most synthetic fertilizers release nutrients into the soil all at once, even if labeled "slow release." Sometimes the release is too fast, so the plants can't absorb the nutrients efficiently, and some of the nutrients get washed away. These fertilizers can burn plants if they're applied incorrectly. Synthetics usually only provide nitrogen, phosphorus, and potassium. Few of them add other nutrients, and none of them contribute texture-improving elements to the soil.

Cover crops, also called green manure, are crops that are grown for a season and then tilled into the soil. They tend to be used on empty vegetable or annual beds. Cover crops have deep roots, and their root action opens the soil up to increase the air in the soil. As they decompose, they release nitrogen into the soil and *add* rather than deplete nutrients. Many different types of cover crops are available. For instance, URI Cooperative Extension Master Gardener Anneliese Williams in West Greenwich plants oats and winter rye, while her colleague Rudi Hempe in Narragansett plants rye and hairy vetch.

Compost, sometimes called "black gold," is the perfect organic amendment. It's a tonic for the garden. Compost improves soil texture, the ability of the soil to retain moisture and nutrients, minerals, and micronutrients. You can also fertilize your plants with a solution called compost tea. "Making compost tea is not a matter of just soaking compost in water, however," says ecological landscape designer Sanne Kure-Jensen of Portsmouth. "It's a little more complicated than that, because you want live microbes." There's a terrific online article from *Fine Gardening* magazine about making compost tea; visit www.taunton.com/ finegardening. Kure-Jensen notes that research is under way to develop a compost tea with a shelf life.

Other amendments. A wonderful gardener friend in Massachusetts, retired certified arborist Barbara Emeneau, adds natural clay kitty litter to improve her sandy soil's water-holding capability. Clay kitty litter is inexpensive and easy to find.

But one of the best amendments is chopped leaves. When I worked at Blithewold Mansion, Gardens & Arboretum in Bristol, we added shredded leaves, compost, and a slow-release organic amendment to the soil every year. The resulting soil in the gardens is soft, dark, crumbly, and moist. You can almost hear the plants sighing happily.

How to Compost

There are various schools of thought about composting. They range from the philosophy that "compost happens" to red wiggler worm composting systems to intricate three-bin managed systems. The system you favor depends on how quickly you want your compost. Or you can try multiple systems, like Rich Pederson, who operates fourteen compost areas in a range of styles at the certified organic City Farm in Providence.

Simple piles are effective, but you have to wait a while. You stack the material and let Mother Nature do the work. If you're in no hurry, then this is the simplest way to go—no work, no management, no fuss.

Worm bins using red wigglers (*Eisenia fetida* or *Lumbricus rubellus*) can be set up in the house, the basement, or the garage. The process is called vermiculture and the end product is vermicompost. The worms eat kitchen scraps, and you collect their nutrient-rich castings to enrich the garden. Rhode Island's own Worm Ladies of Charlestown, Lois Fulton and Nancy Warner, have made a successful business rearing red wigglers and educating the public about them (see chapter 12). "These worms multiply at a rate of knots," says Fulton, "so you'll always have them and be able to give them away to friends." You can also add them to an outdoor compost pile.

The three-bin system requires forking the compost from one bin to the next to the next. It's actually a three-year system. You

Town Compost vs. Home Compost

Municipal composting sites are a source of compost, although you don't always know what you're getting. Ecological landscape architect Chuck Carberry of Providence-based Eco-Tōpe Landscape Design cautions that if towns do not screen the compost, you may find inorganic trash included. And if the town incorporates a lot of yard waste like leaves and grass, you may get toxic chemicals from herbicides that won't break down. "When it comes to taking compost from the site, look for assurance that the compost is good," he says. He recommends that you not use town compost on vegetable gardens just in case it contains residual pesticides. To find a registered town compost site in your area, go to the Rhode Island Resource Recovery Web site at www.rirrc.org or the Rhode Island Department of Environmental Management's Office of Waste Management at www.dem.ri.gov.

harvest the third year's compost for your garden as you tend to the second-year bin and add fresh material to the first-year bin.

Good compost is a balance of "browns" and "greens" layered to ensure efficient decomposition and a good mix at the end. The browns are carbon-rich dry materials like straw, sawdust, dry grass clippings, and leaves. The greens are the nitrogen-rich materials like fresh grass clippings, eggshells, fresh manure, kitchen scraps, and human hair. (Don't add dairy products and meats to your pile. It's not that they're actually bad for the compost, they just take longer to break down, can attract rodents, and make your compost smell bad.)

It is possible to have bad compost, says Mike Merner, owner of the certified organic Earth Care Farm in Charlestown (www.earthcarefarm.com), where he produces premium compost. "Not all compost is equal," he says. "Compost made with diseased plants, weed seeds, or a bad mix of organic material won't be good for your garden." He suggests testing compost at the same place your soil is tested. Merner tests every finished batch he makes, and the pH is always in the 6.9 to 7.2 range. He maintains that what sets his compost apart is the ingredients: "I use animal manures, of course, but it's the ocean products—fish, seaweed, and clamshells—that make it so nutrient rich." The clamshells act as a slow-release form of lime, which is a real boon for Rhode Island gardeners.

Good compost needs to be managed: aerated and moistened. If it's not composting properly, the mixture is probably too dry. If it smells it may be too wet. "Aerating the piles provides oxygen to microorganisms that help rot the organic matter," says Merner. He has been making his black gold for twenty-five years and is diligent about managing the piles. "We have a man on a payloader forty-four hours a week turning the piles and adding water if it hasn't rained."

You say you don't have the space or patience to compost? You can buy composts and manures in bags at your local garden center. You can find locally made compost at the Rhode Island Resource Conservation & Development Council's Web site (www.rircd.org), which lists companies like Merner's Earth Care Farm. And there are new lines of dehydrated composts that are lightweight, easy to spread, and can be used as a mulch. Coast of Maine Organic Products (www.coastofmaine.com) has an excellent product line.

Soils high in organic matter retain much more water. Many towns are urging home owners and contractors to incorporate more compost into lawns and landscapes as a way of conserving water. "A town with 5,000 residences each with 10,000 square feet of lawn could potentially save 94 million gallons of water as a result of increased organic matter in the soil," says Alyson McCann, director of University of Rhode Island's Home*A*Syst Program (www.healthylandscapes.org).

Making compost is therapeutic. Your kitchen scraps feed your garden, the plants that didn't make it (providing they were not sick or diseased) are reborn as compost, and your leaves and grass clippings are put back to work. Nothing goes to waste, and you contribute to the cycle of life. What better way to create good soil and feel good at the same time.

The Site

Soil is only one element of a garden. You can improve your soil and even push the envelope of your growing seasons, but what you can't do is fight the site. Wherever you live in Rhode Island, you have to learn to love your land—marshy, sandy, wind-blown, salty—even rocky wetland like that in North Scituate or the granite ledges, clay soil, and cold up around Foster and Burrillville. Unless you already have perfection—perfect land and perfect soil—or the money to truck in magnificent loam, the land you have is the land you garden on. It's your challenge to make of it a bountiful garden of beauty and plenty.

Know Your Zone

Temperatures directly affect what you can grow—and elevation influences temperatures. Even though Rhode Island doesn't have mountains, it does have Jerimoth Hill in the northwest of the state at 812 feet above sea level. Elevation variations are one cause of temperature differences in the state. In general, for every 250 feet above sea level the temperature drops 1 degree Fahrenheit. Folks near the water in Narragansett will be gardening in temperatures that could be nearly 4 degrees warmer than Burrillville. Just a few degrees can mean the difference between frost and no frost and between what survives the winter and what succumbs.

Here's where knowing your hardiness zone can be enormously helpful.

In 1960 the United States Department of Agriculture (USDA) mapped the country into areas, or zones, based on a 10-degree Fahrenheit difference in average annual minimum temperatures for each zone. These zones are called USDA Hardiness Zones and are used to identify which plants will survive low temperature. The zones range from Zone 1, with an annual minimum temperature of minus 50 degrees, to Zone 10, with an annual minimum temperature of 35 to 40 degrees. The map was revised and updated in 1990 to include subzones, like 5a and 5b, and an additional Zone 11, which represents minimum temperatures above 40 degrees. The 1990 version of the USDA Hardiness Zone map is usually what appears in books. You can view the map online at the United States National Arboretum Web site (www.usna.usda.gov/Hardzone/ushzmap.html) or, for a clearer view, at the *Better Homes & Gardens* Web site (www.bhg.com).

New Zones Coming

The first hardiness zone map was published in 1927 by the Arnold Arboretum and had eight zones. Most recently, gardeners have been following the 1990 U.S. Department of Agriculture Hardiness Zone map. But changes in weather, airflow patterns, and the effect of water and heat on the land have necessitated an update of the USDA Hardiness Zone map. Watch for the release of a new USDA map, which will reorganize the zones so that there will be fifteen zones instead of the current eleven and no subzones.

Until this new USDA map arrives, the map prepared in 2006 by the National Arbor Day Foundation is now appearing in some publications. Based on fifteen years of data, the Arbor Day map bumps up a lot of current USDA zones into a warmer temperature zone. You can find the map online at www.arborday.org.

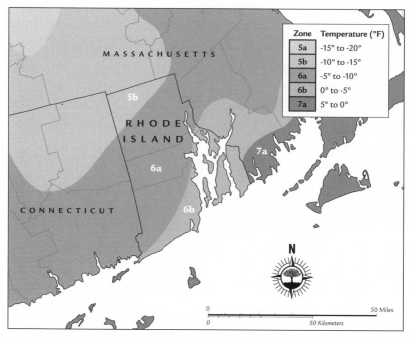

The map legend reads:

Zone	Temperature (°F)
5a	-15° to -20°
5b	-10° to -15°
6a	-5° to -10°
6b	0° to -5°
7a	5° to 0°

USDA Hardiness Zones for Rhode Island

Hardiness zones are not a complete catalog of your area's growing conditions. They are guides, not gospel. But they are one of the best predictors of whether a plant will survive in your garden over the winter. The nursery and landscaping industry uses the information from the USDA map to rate and label its plants for hardiness. Knowing your USDA Hardiness Zone is useful when buying plants, but there are other factors involved in whether a plant lives or dies in your garden—microclimates, or pockets of warm or cold temperatures, being a key factor. Many landscape professionals and gardeners advise taking hardiness zone designations with a grain of salt. Beth Rowe of Block Island says that because of winter freezes and thaws, she can't plant anything marked Zone 6 or 7 and expect it to be hardy out there. "If I stick with Zone 5, the plants survive," she says. So, the long and the short of it is, be aware of your assigned hardiness zone, but don't rely on it solely.

Rhode Island Zones

The Ocean State is *primarily* USDA Hardiness Zone 6 (incorporating 6a and 6b) through the center of the state, but there is a triangle of 5b in the northwest corner and a swath of 7a in the east and along the coast. No single county is just one zone! Providence County, for instance, is mostly 6a with a blip of 5b in the upper northernmost corner. Kent and Washington Counties are split almost in half between 6a and 6b, Bristol is 6b, and Newport County is split between 6b and 7a.

Here are the Rhode Island zones and what they mean in terms of the average annual minimum temperatures:

Zone 5b ($-10°F$ to $-15°F$): Up in Burrillville, parts of Glocester and maybe a little of Foster

Zone 6a ($-5°F$ to $-10°F$): From Woonsocket in the north down to Exeter and some of Hopkinton in the southwest

Zone 6b ($0°F$ to $-5°F$): A swath from Pawtucket down through Barrington and Bristol, and all the way down to the southern coast and Block Island

Zone 7a ($0°F$ to $5°F$): Narragansett, Aquidneck Island, and toward Tiverton and Little Compton

Heat Zones

Hot weather affects plants, too. Plants may not react to increasing temperatures immediately, as they would to a sudden frost, but over days or weeks high temperatures can kill. To address this issue the American Horticultural Society created the AHS Heat Zone Map. It gives you another dimension of knowledge about your site. Find the map online at www.ahs.org/publications/heat_zone_map.htm, where you can also purchase a poster of the map.

Frost Dates and Your Growing Season

Hardiness zone ratings predict which plants will survive your lowest temperatures, but the zones don't tell you when those low temperatures occur. Your "growing season" is defined as the number of days between the last frost of the spring and the first frost of the fall. Your growing season, or "frost-free days," will determine when to plant out in the spring and when to cease garden cultivation in the fall.

Two USDA maps—the last spring frost map and the first autumn frost map—give general frost dates for the United States: The last frost in Rhode Island is estimated to occur from April 1 to April 30 and the first frost from November 1 to 30. You have to dig deeper to unearth the frost dates for your area. For freeze and frost data from locations around the state, check the Web site of the National Weather Service at www.nws.noaa.gov. The URI Cooperative Extension Master Gardeners provide a vegetable planting guide on their Web site (www.urimga.org), which is based on a final frost of May 15 and a first frost of October 15.

Below are some typical frost dates pulled from the National Oceanic and Atmospheric Administration Web site (www.noaa.gov). Consider these dates to be general guidelines only. Readings posted on the site are commonly made at a height of 5 feet, and actual ground temperature can be 4 to 8 degrees less. Ground frost can occur even when the measured air temperature is 36 degrees. Site specifics, radiational cooling, air drainage, and other factors will influence actual frost dates at your location, the NOAA site says.

	Typical last frost (spring)	Typical first frost (fall)
Block Island	April 20	October 29
Kingston	May 20	September 27
Foster	May 30	September 3

As you can see, frost dates vary greatly around the state, resulting in a different number of frost-free days and therefore different growing seasons. Frank Crandall, owner of Wood River Evergreens in Hope Valley, experienced five hard frosts in his area by November 4 in 2006. Organic grower Jayne Merner Senecal at Earth Care Farm in Charlestown has had a last frost as late as June 5 and a first as early as September 9. "I can't plant frost-tender seedlings outside until June," she says.

The only way you can *really* know the frost dates in your exact location is to start keeping your own records or check with your local garden centers to see if they have kept records. And talk to your neighbors.

Documented Weather Data for Rhode Island

- Average annual minimum temperature: –10°F to 0°F

- Average dates of last spring frost: April 1–April 30

- Average date of first fall frost: September 15–October 30

- Average temperature in January: 29°F

- Average temperature in July: 72°F

- Spring: March 15–May 15

- Fall: September 15–November 1

Types of Frost

We all know that frost occurs at 32 degrees Fahrenheit. But there are in fact three different categories of frost:

Light freeze: 32 to 36 degrees. Tender plants are killed, but not much harm is done to other plants.

Moderate or normal freeze: 28 to 32 degrees. This will destroy most annuals and cause particular damage to fruit blossoms and to tender and semihardy plants. It will also kill off the tops of perennials and may damage some shallow-rooted perennials.

Hard or severe freeze: 28 degrees. This will kill susceptible plants outright. At these temperatures the ground freezes solid, with the depth of the freeze dependent on the length of the freeze, soil moisture, and soil type.

Frost does not *have* to determine the beginning and end of your growing season. Folks who garden in the northwest, colder areas of Rhode Island may want to extend and protect their harvest, whereas the folks in southern Rhode Island, where it's warmer, may only need to see the season out.

Extending your growing season means capturing the sun's warmth for as long as you can. You do this by diligently protecting crops. Floating row covers, movable greenhouses, temporary hoop houses, cold frames, cloches, hot caps, and mulch are all devices to retain warmth so that plants can grow more quickly in spring and keep growing after autumn frost. Heavy mulching can help warm the soil in spring and retain heat and moisture in the fall. Shredded leaves, seaweed, and salt hay are great winter mulches. Just remember to lift the heavy winter mulch in the spring to help the soil warm up and get things moving in the garden. Lighten up on the mulch during the growing season.

Of course, you can defy the cold and grow plants year-round if you really want, but that requires a lot of effort and protection for your crops. Eliot Coleman's *The Four Season Harvest* thoroughly details how to do this. Another marvelous book on the subject is *A Gardener's Guide to Frost: Outwit the Weather and Extend the Spring and Fall Seasons,* by Philip Harnden.

The Specifics of Your Site

How well do you know your garden's weather and climate? "Weather" means atmospheric conditions like heat, cold, rain (or lack of), wind, and snow. "Climate" refers to those particular conditions that happen in a specific region. *Your* climate is the weather in your area, or even your garden. John Ghiorse, NBC/WJAR Channel 10's meteorologist and an avid gardener, is often quoted as saying that "all weather is local." He maintains that it's hard to forecast weather in Rhode Island because the state has so many wildcard elements: ocean, bay, highland, valleys, and inland water. "You can't believe you're in the same state when driving from Burrillville to Newport in one day," he says. "The weather can be *so* different!"

Knowing your own property intimately is every bit as important as knowing what area of the state you live in and its general hardiness and heat zones. "The right plant in the right place" is the enduring mantra. Plants that adapt to your situation will be the easiest to grow. Different plants need different growing conditions: Vegetables love full sun all day, so a happy vegetable garden would be on a gentle slope facing south, with good water drainage, protected from the harsh winds but with just the right amount of airflow. Perennials can handle varied conditions. Some thrive in shade, partial shade, or full sun; others celebrate damp situations.

Before you plant your garden, assess your property's topographical features, orientation, sun exposure, wind exposure, air-flow, microclimates, water drainage, existing plantings, views, and location of property lines and utilities.

Topography

Learning the topography of the state, and of your corner of the state, can help you understand your own site. The western part of Rhode Island is part of the New England uplands, and the eastern part of the state belongs to the lowlands of the Narragansett Bay. The bay features prominently in the state's topography.

Once you have a sense of your local terrain, look at the specifics of your property. Is it on a steep hill? Is it gently sloping or flat? Or is it a combination of hill and flatland? Is it on a rocky coast or in a valley? If you have hills you may need to grade, build terraced beds, or landscape steps into the side of the hill to retain soil and water. If you have completely flat land, you may need to ensure good drainage so that water doesn't pool and create soggy conditions inhospitable to plants you want to grow.

Topographical features include things like rivers, lakes, ponds, or swamps. If you have an overly damp garden, you may be able to construct a pond, water feature, or bog. There are plants for every situation—John Phillip Jr. of Narragansett, a URI CE Master Gardener, formed the New England Carnivorous Plant Society to encourage more folks to grow these plants on their soggy land (www.necps.org).

Orientation and Sun Exposure

Track the sun through the day and through a year and record how the sun changes its angle and direction in your garden hour by hour and season by season. Locate south to orient vegetable beds for optimum sun exposure. You may want to create a shade garden on the north side of the house or a perennial bed on the east side that gets sun half the day. Again, there are plants for every situation.

Airflow and Wind

Air flows downhill in the same way water flows downhill. If your garden is on the side of a hill, the air will flow through it, which is good. If your garden is at the top of the hill, the air may batter the plants. If it's at the bottom of the hill, your plants may "drown" in a pool of cold air. A breeze is a positive—a howling wind is not. Farm manager Mike Hutchison at Casey Farm in Saunderstown maintains that it is the wind that delays their spring every year.

Air needs to flow through a garden for the health of the plants but not so forcefully that it pounds them. Keep the air moving. You may need to divert the airflow by clearing a path and redirecting it by means of a built structure or strategically planted shrubs. Windbreaks need to be permeable so that air can flow through and should not be so high as to cut down on available sunshine. And just as you track the sun's seasonal movements, track the wind through the seasons. You may not need windbreaks year-round.

Microclimates

A microclimate is the weather and climate in a small pocket or area of your property or neighborhood. Even though the USDA Hardiness Zone map assigns Zone 6b to your locale, for instance, you may have areas on your property that defy the zone for any number of reasons. For example, Karin Welt of the Well Tended Garden in Cumberland was lifting dahlias in mid-November, after several frosts, and she noticed a cluster of dahlias in full bloom in a south-facing alcove. "The area is bordered by a cement sidewalk and a row of arborvitae," she explains, which created a microclimate where the plants could defy frost.

Microclimates occur naturally or you can create them. You

can exploit your site's microclimates to extend your growing season or the sequence of bloom. Jayne Merner Senecal's property is tucked in the forest of the great swamp of Charlestown, and it gets very little wind. "Frost-hardy seedlings do great here," she says. "The tree-lined fields protect the seedlings from spring's harsh gusts." Senecal seeds her first round of peas, spinach, and lettuce on St. Patrick's Day, which is two to four weeks earlier than most. "I am the first with spring produce at the markets."

You may have a completely exposed garden on a hillside subject to harsh winds. You had all but given up gardening there until you put in a windbreak of trees and shrubs. Or you may have a sun trap created by a wall of your house in conjunction with a nearby hedge, as does Beth Rowe out on the Block, where the plants are toasty warm and sheltered even when the wind howls elsewhere through the garden. It can be fun to try to defy hardiness zones, but unless you have the perfect microclimates, you may be disappointed. To lessen your chances of zonal disappointment, use the zone map as a guide.

Water and Drainage

Note how water behaves on your property. Go out in your garden during a rainstorm and watch how the water moves across your land. Low spots can be discerned much more easily in the rain. Then use your property's natural qualities to your advantage.

Track rainfall in your garden with a simple rain gauge. You can also get state-specific rainfall statistics from the National Weather Service at www.nws.noaa.gov.

Existing Plantings

What you inherit on your land could be gorgeous—or not. Old foundation plantings may need to be ripped out to make way for new ones. You may have beautiful old trees or ugly trees that shade too much of the garden and need to be pruned or cut down.

The plants you inherit—including the weeds!—are indicators

of what grows well in your garden. A friend of mine found native Solomon's seals (*Polygonatum biflorum*) and lady ferns (*Athyrium felix-femina*) on her property. These plants do well in dry woodland, which is what she has. She says that if she had really taken note of these existing plants, she wouldn't have tried—and failed—with woodland plants that need moister conditions.

Views

You may want to enhance naturally beautiful views to the ocean or block out an eyesore next door. Assess the lines of sight—the view from the house to the road, the view from the road to the house, the view out to your perennial bed or your vegetable garden or your pond. All these should be factored in when planning where to locate your beds and other plantings. Bear in mind that beautiful open views may herald problems with wind.

Property Lines and Utilities

An official surveyor's map will show demarcations of your property and the location of your septic system, power, and utility lines. You don't want to plant your favorite specimen tree on someone else's property or right under a power line.

All in all, get to know your land and build a relationship with it. Anne Wilson of Newport has for many years maintained a garden on a private estate just off Ocean Drive and facing the Atlantic Ocean. It's not an easy site because it's very windy. But she shrugs off the challenge and says that every garden has its quirks: "You just have to read it all—soil, climate. Every part has its own microclimate."

Part of the fun of gardening is working with what you have. You can create a wonderful gardening experience whatever the features of your site. Enhance the existing positive conditions and minimize the negative aspects of your property. That's the challenge—and the joy.

Water

Everyone knows that all plants need water to grow. But how much water to apply, and how often to apply it, is tricky to assess. Some plants need very little moisture, while others want to be swamped. It's crucial to know the water needs of the plants you want to grow. Selecting plants that can adapt to your watering practices is important, too. If you're not good about remembering to water, then don't grow plants that need a constant supply of moisture!

The overall average rainfall for Rhode Island is 45 inches per year. But not every year is the same—in 1998, for instance, it was more like 62 inches. And there are swaths and pockets around the state where the averages differ. In the center to the west, between the Flat River Reservoir and the Usquepaug and Wood Rivers, the average can be as much as 65 inches annually. Clearly your need for supplemental watering will be different if you live there rather than, say, on Prudence Island or in West Greenwich, which generally get less precipitation.

Various factors affect how much you need to water:

Temperature can differ as much as 15 degrees around the state. In one trip from Woonsocket to Newport to Westerly you will feel the difference in air temperature. Warmer temperatures cause soil to dry more quickly than cooler temperatures.

Wind can be desiccating. A garden on a windy hilltop in Scituate may dry out as easily as a garden near a windswept beach on Block Island.

The type of soil in your garden affects how much water you need. Clay soils tend to get waterlogged, and sandy soils tend to drain too well. Soil drainage translates to how well water is transmitted through the surface soil and subsoil. Most landscape plants, fruit trees, and berry bushes need good drainage to a depth of at least 2 feet. If your garden does not drain well and water pools on-site, you may want to garden in raised beds as do a lot of folks in Watch Hill. Creating drainage systems such as gravel pits or seepage pits are expensive alternatives.

How Much to Water

Disease and mineral deficiencies can exhibit similar-looking symptoms to those of overwatering or underwatering. If your plants are looking less than wonderful, do a little research before you throw water at them.

The goal in watering sensibly is to make sure your garden gets adequately watered without overwatering, underwatering, or wasting water. You need to know how much water each plant needs. A large tree may draw up as much as 400 gallons of water a day from the soil and release it into the atmosphere through the process of *transpiration*. Overwatering is both harmful to plants, wasteful, and expensive. It can cause root and fungal diseases, create a habitat for slugs and snails, and wash nutrients from the soil. Plants can drown if there is too much water in the soil. On the other hand, plants struggle to absorb nutrients from dry soil, so underwatering leads to smaller flowers and fruit, weaker plants, and dehydration.

Water long, deep, and infrequently. The rule of thumb is to give your garden 1 inch of water a week all at one time but slowly—about ½ inch an hour—so that the water has a chance to soak in. That 1 inch of water *should* wet the soil down to 12 inches, but check by digging down 1 foot with a trowel. It might take a long time to saturate partched soil. If you water for half an hour and then dig into the soil to find it's wet only to ½ inch deep, then you know your soil requires a longer watering session.

Infrequent but long and deep watering will encourage deep rooting. Frequent light watering encourages shallow rooting. Roots look for water, and if water is on the surface only, then that's where the roots stay. Adjust water to the needs of the plant.

Rainwater Harvesting Demonstration Park

The Bristol County Water Authority is creating a rainwater harvesting project to demonstrate how harvested rainwater from the roof of a public building will support the water needs in a small community park. "Sustainable gardening will be practiced, and sustainable gardening instruction will be provided to the community gardeners," says Susan Andrade, engineering technician with the BCWA. The project will run rainwater harvesting workshops conducted by URI Cooperative Extension Master Gardeners. For information call (401) 245-2033.

Roses, for instance, may require as much as five to eight gallons a week. Some experts recommend watering for as much as two to three hours every two weeks, particularly for newly planted trees. And never allow seedlings to dry out because they probably won't recover.

Measure the amount of rainwater and sprinkler water received by your garden by placing a rain gauge in the soil or attaching it to a low post. If your garden is on different levels, use gauges throughout, because your garden may not be getting the same amount of water everywhere.

When the soil is truly wet, stop watering.

The University of Rhode Island's Home*A*Syst Program provides information for home owners about sustainable gardening and water use. It has a wonderful Web site with a host of information about watering wisely, rain barrels, harvesting water, rain gardens, and more. Visit www.healthylandscapes.org. Notes Alyson McCann, the program's director: "Residential water use can increase 50 percent or more in the summer due to outdoor uses, much of which is used on lawns and gardens." According to the National Irrigation Association, most home owners overwater their yard. "Each of us can adopt practices that conserve our water," McCann adds.

When to Water

Water when the plants need to be watered—not because the calendar says you should or simply because you haven't watered for a while. Check the condition of your garden. Maybe the sun hasn't been shining or temperatures have been lower than normal and the garden hasn't dried out enough to need water. Many plants require less moisture water once they are fully established. (This may take up to three years in the case of trees.)

The optimum time for watering is early morning, because that gives the plants many hours to absorb the water before temperatures rise and the water evaporates. The next best time to water is in late afternoon, when the leaves still have a chance to dry off before the cooler temperatures of the evening. If you leave the watering until evening, temperatures may drop while the garden is still wet and create damp conditions loved by diseases and slugs, snails, and other pests.

It is inefficient to water in the middle of the day when temperatures are at their highest. This is wasteful and there are no rewards for the plants. At best much of the water may simply evaporate, at worst the water beads act as magnifying lenses that burn the leaves.

Having said all of that, it is better to water your plants when you can, even if it's not the best time to do so, rather than not watering at all. We're all very busy and get to tasks when we are able. Just be aware of the problems associated with watering at less than optimum times.

Water Wisely

The most efficient way to water is to apply moisture to the roots where it is most needed—that is, apply water directly to the soil and not onto the foliage. That way water will arrive exactly where it can be absorbed and will not linger on the leaves and encourage disease.

- Roots of annuals are typically in the top 12 inches of soil.

- The root system of trees and shrubs may go down a couple of feet and extend two to five times the spread of the branches, but the feeder roots are close to the surface if not actually on the surface.

- Root systems of lawns are typically only 4 to 6 inches deep.

Use a watering system that directs water to the roots most efficiently. You don't want to spray your asphalt driveway, deck, pathways, house. . . . Fortunately you can choose from many effective watering systems.

Hand Watering

Watering with a watering can or a hose can be therapeutic. It gets you in touch with your garden so you can check how things are growing and look for problems. But to deeply hand water any portion of your garden would mean standing there for a very long time. Better to keep your hand watering for containers and small beds. If you like to hand water, one method you can use is to sink perforated containers into the soil next to a plant. Fill the container and it will distribute water slowly directly to the root system. This is particularly good if you notice one or two plants that are looking a little droopy. You won't water everything just because of the needs of a few.

As with any watering system, handheld or not, check to make sure the garden is being watered correctly. Dig into soil one hour after watering to check soil moisture depth.

Sprinklers

There are many types of sprinklers: overhead, stationary, pulsating or impulse, rotary, and oscillating. Some sprinklers are hard to adjust for range or direction, and you'll find yourself watering areas that don't need it—the front porch, your car in the driveway. . . . Any sprinkler that keeps the water close to the ground is more efficient because there's less chance for evaporation. Some sprinklers are better for different areas of the garden. I particularly like noodle-head sprinklers because I can direct the spray exactly where I want it.

Overhead sprinklers spray water high overhead. The disadvantage of overheads is that some water will evaporate before it reaches the ground.

Impulse or pulsating sprinklers operate on lower water pressure yet can discharge more water over a greater area than other sprinklers. You adjust the spray to reach only the target area, which is a more efficient use of water. The spray is strong and close to the ground, so it is wind resistant. The stream can also be adjusted from full jet to fine mist.

Automatic sprinkler systems have one big disadvantage: They're automatic. Sure, you don't have to be around to switch them on and off, but people don't always take the time to override the automatic features when plants don't need water. As the seasons change so too do the moisture requirements of plants, and the sprinkler system should be reprogrammed. It's also important to install a rain shutoff device for automatic systems. These systems can be complicated to program and require maintenance. Part of the system may stop working and you'll have uneven watering—and you may not even notice until part of your lawn or garden dies.

Soaker Hoses

Soaker hoses "sweat" water out along their entire length. They are made of a porous material that allows water to soak or weep through directly to the soil. Winding the hoses through the beds, spacing them to get as close to plants as possible to treat plants evenly.

Water pressure may be a factor with soaker hoses. Don't make the hoses so long that water can't make it to the end, otherwise plants far from the faucet get shortchanged. By using a Y connector at the faucet, you can have several shorter hoses watering at the same time.

Drip Irrigation

Drip irrigation gets water directly to the soil through tiny outlets called emitters. Drip irrigation hoses are laid on the ground between plants or installed under the soil. It's easier to detect a problem when the hoses are above ground, but the hoses are not attractive and may look better covered with mulch or leaves. The hoses are carefully placed to ensure even watering of all plants. It is easier to match plant needs and soil types with a drip system, particularly in large or sloped areas where water pressure may make soaker-hose output erratic.

Rain Barrels

Although not technically a watering system, rain barrels are good supplements to other watering tools. With a rain barrel you can "harvest" or catch rainwater—which is naturally soft water with no chlorine, fluoride, minerals, and other chemicals—and store that water for later use. Rainwater is what plants like most. A rain barrel can be a plain old barrel or a fancy one made of plastic and equipped

When to Water

You know it's time to water when . . .

- Soil is dry below the surface.

- Wilted leaves on trees and shrubs will not perk up in the evening.

- Leaves on trees turn yellow and drop before the fall.

- Lawns are a dull green and footprints show.

- It's difficult to push a screwdriver or trowel into the soil.

with mesh screens, brass spigots, bottom drains, overflow valves, and hose connectors. A rain barrel's capacity is usually sixty to eighty gallons. The best location for the barrel is under a roof downspout. If possible install the barrel at a height above where you want to water to give you some water pressure. If you have no pressure, you can either use this water in watering cans or install an inexpensive pump to get it moving.

Make sure your barrel has a cover to prevent debris from collecting, to prevent pets or even children from falling in, and to discourage mosquitoes. URI CE Master Gardener Ann Perkins in Narragansett adds a little fertilizer to the water in her barrels so she always has a supply of "high-octane" water for her plants, particularly her containers. She is careful, however, to keep the "octane" dilute so she doesn't overfertilize.

Using harvested rainwater is a great way to save money, too, because you're not using municipal water. Finding rain barrels is easy. A Web site that provides in-depth information about rain barrels with links to suppliers is www.rainbarrelguide.com. Sometimes the URI Cooperative Extension Master Gardener program will guide you to suppliers, or they may set up a bulk rain-barrel purchase system. The university's Home*A*Syst Web site (www.healthylandscapes.org) is also helpful.

Intelligent Irrigation

If you have plenty of rainfall and are in no danger of going without water, then you are a lucky gardener. Most of us experience periods of drought during the summer and must conserve water and irrigate intelligently. Remember, whether you are using municipal water or water from a well, it's coming from the same place—groundwater reservoirs. During town water bans, some folks think it's fine to use well water to run their sprinkler systems. Using well water is still depleting the same water supply, so maybe it's not so fine.

Your irrigation system can be informal—you and the watering can when needed—or you can get sophisticated with a combination of sprinklers, soaker hoses, and supplemental hand watering. As you make your irrigation plan, consider these approaches:

Build irrigation zones into your design. This means grouping plants with similar water needs together. Choose plants that need minimal water, and remember that many plants require less water once they are established—which could mean after two or three years.

Prioritize what needs to be watered. You may want to place young plants that need extra coddling at the top of your list, or plants that matter the most to you, or simply the ones that really need more water.

Mulch to conserve water. A 2- to 4-inch layer of organic mulch will conserve water and reduce weeds. Compost is the best mulch because it adds nutrients to the soil, unlike bark chips that can reduce some nutrients, or stone mulch that adds no nutrients. Mark Kimball and his gardening friends out on Prudence Island swear by seaweed. "There's nothing better as a mulch," he says. "And don't rinse it—you'll wash off all the good stuff." Buckwheat hulls are also a favorite mulch because they allow water to pass through without absorbing any of the water. "Keep mulch from touching plant stems," says ecological landscape designer Sanne Kure-Jensen. "Always leave a gap of a few

> ## Drought Watch
>
> The U.S. Geological Survey works with federal, state, and other agencies to compile water use estimates for counties in the United States. You can get an overall picture of how much water is used in your area, and see the differences around the state, at www.usgs.gov; look under Drought Watch. Or track dry conditions through the drought-monitoring Web site set up by the USDA and the National Drought Mitigation Center: http://drought.unl.edu/dm/monitor.

Water-Wise Tips

- Dig to loosen the soil and encourage water absorption. Try not to dig in dry weather because the soil dries out fast.

- Weeds compete for water and nutrients. Keep up with the weeding.

- Shelter plants from drying winds, and shade seedlings.

- Use gray water wherever possible. This is recycled household water from your shower, rinsed dishes, or any previous use of water that does not leave the water contaminated with bacteria or detergents.

inches between tree trunk and the mulch to deter disease, rot, rodents, and insects."

Minimize runoff. Create berms or swales around plants to contain water. Carefully water sloped areas to ensure the plants are actually getting watered. You may want to terrace so that water stays put or to build diversions that harvest runoff.

Divert roof runoff to spread over well-drained soil. Use porous paving materials on driveways and walkways so that runoff is reabsorbed back into the groundwater supply.

Plant individual plants in trenches and bowls. Build soil ridges to hold water right in the root zone. Using a hose or watering can, flood the root zones so you're only watering the plants and not the weeds in between.

Improve soils with amendments. Conditioning soil greatly enhances the soil's ability to absorb and hold water. Soil with high organic content needs to be irrigated less even under hot, dry conditions.

Husband and wife Earle and Ann Perkins in Wakefield, both URI CE Master Gardeners, have devised numerous ways of coping with water issues on their rocky, uneven piece of Rhode Island. "We live on a rock!" laughs Ann. "Water runs right off our property without watering anything." But they have created a spectacular destination garden by deliberately designing their garden to retain moisture. They use mulch and compost to improve the water retention of the soil and have built berms and swales to retain and channel water. They have also planted for erosion control using hostas and daylilies.

Xeriscaping in Rhode Island

Xeriscaping is the term used for landscaping with indigenous and drought-tolerant plants that, once established, are particularly adapted to going without much water. It is also a way of conserving water. Xeric plants are happy in a dry garden.

A xeric garden isn't going to look like a lush, moist English cottage garden, says ecological landscape architect Chuck Carberry of Eco-Tōpe Landscape Design in Providence. "Expect some drying and desiccation. And don't pamper the area, otherwise it will never build the xeric qualities." Here are some of his xeriscaping tips and techniques:

- Choose your plants carefully—the right plant for your conditions.

- You may need to water initially as the plant is getting established. But once the roots enter the soil, you will build the plants' independence from water by leaving them alone.

- Allow drying to occur to build xeric characteristics in the plant.

- If a plant is suffering from lack of water, don't pamper it—allow it to die and replace it with new plants, Carberry asserts. You will end up with a site established with xeric plants.

- Plant windbreaks to cut down on damage from drying winds.

- Be sure the plants are properly nourished, especially with potassium, which aids in water conservation.

- And mulch to conserve water.

Drought-Tolerant Plants

When the question "What plants have you used that seem to cope with droughty conditions?" was raised around the state, a resoundingly similar list came back. Julie Medeiros in Cumberland, Dee Scamacca in Scituate, Paula Mottshaw in Foster, and Mary Anne Brady in Barrington offered these proven recommendations.

- Black-eyed Susan (*Rudbeckia*)
- Cotoneaster
- Ornamental grasses
- Purple coneflower (*Echinacea*)
- Russian sage (*Perovskia*)
- Spirea
- Spurge (*Euphorbia cyparissias*)
- Stonecrop (*Sedum* 'Autumn Joy')

"One important thing to remember is any plant that is said to be 'drought tolerant' is so only once established. It does *not* mean plant it and never water it," asserts landscape designer Linda Hughes in Narragansett. For low maintenance and drought tolerance she favors anything in the Mediterranean garden line: artemisia, *Genista* (broom), rock rose, helichrysum, hardy prickly pear, yucca, viburnums, salvias, dianthus, digitalis, Shasta daisy, lavender, poppies, many of the grasses, and all the sedums.

Plants with Wet Feet

For the folks who get abundant rainfall, particularly those in central western Rhode Island, here are plants that prefer to have wet feet. First we look at the recommendations from John Holscher of the Good Earth organic garden center (www.goodearthorganic gardencenter.com) in Hope:

Cardinal flower (*Lobelia cardinalis*). Red! "A native plant and hummingbird favorite," says Holscher. Cardinal flower reseeds freely. Part to full shade.

False spirea (*Astilbe* spp.). White, pink, or red feathery flowers borne above ferny foliage. Usually prefers part sun, depending on the species.

Joe-pye weed (*Eupatorium maculatum*). A native beauty with large pink flowers in late summer. Part to full sun.

Marsh marigold (*Caltha palustris*). A native plant with rounded green leaves and bright yellow, buttercup-like flowers. Sun to part shade.

Meadowsweet (*Filipendula ulmaria*). Lovely ferny foliage with fluffy pink flower plumes. It likes boggy sites but will do well in average garden soil. Part to full sun.

Rodger's flower (*Rodgersia* spp.). Large, often bronze, chestnutlike leaves provide great texture; fragrant, creamy white flowers. Part to full shade.

Royal fern (*Osmunda regalis*). Fronds serve as shelter for ducks and other aquatic creatures, Holscher notes. Sun to part shade.

Sensitive fern (*Onoclea sensibilis*). A native plant with coarsely divided fronds that grows in wet meadows and woods, in swamps, and along stream banks. It's usually found in slightly acidic soil. Part to full sun.

Turtlehead (*Chelone lyonii* or *C. obliqa*). "Pink turtlehead-shaped flowers peek up through dark green foliage in late summer," Holscher states. "A butterfly favorite." Part to full sun.

Windflower (*Anenome* spp.) Dark green divided foliage with lovely pink or white flowers on long stems. Part shade.

For more plants that thrive in wet conditions, we turn to John Phillip Jr., who founded the New England Carnivorous Plant Society (www.necps.org) because he so loves bog plants. His much-visited bog plant display garden at Roger Williams Park Botanical Center is a treasure trove of plants that like wet conditions. It's worth a visit. Here are some of his recommendations:

Blue flag iris (*Iris versicolor*). You may see this plant blooming wild in early summer. It loves wet sites but can handle a bit drier. "Beautiful blue flowers can cover a whole field," Phillip says.

Highbush and lowbush blueberries (*Vaccinum* spp.). These plants provide some fall color, "and what the birds don't eat, you can! Especially try the sweet small lowbush types for lower-growing areas and ground plantings," he notes.

Lady's tresses orchids (*Spiranthes* spp.). "There is something amazingly cool about growing orchids outside at home. The *Spiranthes* in my bog garden bloom from mid-fall through the first mild frosts. Two plants from the Rhode Island Wild Plant Society became ten in just a few years!"

Mountain laurel (*Kalmia* spp.). "Rhododendrons get so much attention, but mountain laurels put on a flowering show that is just as beautiful," says Phillip.

Pitcher plants (*Sarracenia* spp.). "We have one native insectivorous pitcher plant in Rhode Island (*S. purpurea*), but those that grow in the South are also hardy here." These plants feature beautiful, upside-down red, yellow, or white flowers in late spring and early summer. "The white-topped pitcher plant and varieties (*S. leucophylla*) feasts on aggressive yellow jacket wasps!"

Sundews (*Drosera intermedia* and *D. filiformis*). "Two carnivorous plants that like sandy or even fine, gravely soil that stays wet or damp year-round," he notes.

Winterberry (*Ilex verticillata*). "A tall, upright bush with fall color and wonderful bright red berries that jump out in the landscape."

I have yet to venture into the world of bog plants, but every time I talk with Phillip I find myself increasingly intrigued. Plants that love to be in damp conditions are still exotica for me. But until I go down that road, I will continue to faithfully water my own garden—all the while trying to choose plants that don't require too much moisture. I'm mindful of the place water has in our world and try not to waste it.

Green Things

Annuals

I confess to having had a somewhat superior attitude toward annuals when I first started to garden. I didn't think they were as "important" as perennial plants. I learned! Just peruse my huge library of books on gardening and designing with annuals and you'll understand. I now love annuals and their variety: small, mounded flowers; tall, willowy flowers; cheerful plants or those with drama; plants with great foliage; plants that trail or climb; and more. And the names! Farewell-to-spring (*Clarkia*), love-lies-bleeding (*Amaranthus*), or baby-blue-eyes (*Nemophila*). I'm always astonished at the ease and speed with which annuals grow and their energetic flower production.

You can use annuals in so many ways: in containers, as cut flowers, among vegetables, together in annual beds, mixed into perennial beds, clambering up tepees, or sprawling over walls. They come and go in one season, so next year you try something different or replant what you love. You don't have to worry about overwintering these plants through a finicky Rhode Island winter.

An annual germinates, grows to maturity, sets seed, and dies all in one season. In general, annuals are categorized as hardy, half-hardy, or tender.

Hardy annuals are exactly that—tough and hardy. Sow them before the last frost, as soon as the ground can be worked. You can start them indoors a few weeks before the last frost date for earlier bloom. Some can be sown outdoors in fall for spring germination. English marigold (*Calendula officinalis*) or mallow (*Lavatera* *trimestris*) are designated hardy. Hardy annuals are often confused with biennials.

Half-hardy annuals are more sensitive to cold than hardy annuals. They can be started indoors six to eight weeks before the last frost date and set out after the last frost, although they can take a slight frost if your timing isn't perfect. Blanketflower (*Gaillardia)* and gazania are examples of half-hardy annuals.

Tender annuals need TLC. They don't tolerate any cold and will be killed by frost. Start them indoors about ten weeks before the last frost date. Don't put them out until two to three weeks *after* the last frost. In fact, don't plant them until the soil is warm. Impatiens is a tender annual, as is rose moss (*Portulaca grandiflora*).

Some of the plants that we treat as tender annuals in the Ocean State are actually biennials and perennials in other regions or countries. They simply cannot survive the Rhode Island winters. Coleus, impatiens, and some salvias are examples of these plants, which are also known as "tender perennials." Many Rhode Island gardeners use them in their designs as if they were annuals.

Choosing Annuals

When people think of annuals, they usually think of plants that love full sun. Not many annuals like the shade—they may survive in the shade but will probably become weak and leggy. A few that can handle shade include gomphrena (*Gomphrena globosa*) and pincushion flower (*Scabiosa atropurpurea*).

Your choices of annuals are many and varied, and most are easy to grow. Some annuals prefer to be sown directly outside, like coreopsis; others need to be started indoors, like petunias. Some annuals germinate in fewer than ten days, such as ageratum, while others need up to twenty-five days, like Transvaal daisy (*Gerbera lamesonii*).

The great thing about annuals is you're never stuck with a plant you don't like. You can choose different varieties every year. You've probably noticed that in recent years nurseries have

started selling branded selections. Proven Winners and Blooms of Bressingham are just two of the branded selections of plants. Just remember that some branding is marketing, not a completely impartial assessment of plants.

In contrast, All-America Selections (www.all-america selections.org) is a nonprofit organization that *does* evaluate plants impartially. AAS has a network of trial gardens throughout North America where flower and vegetable varieties are grown and assessed. The 2007 winners included *Celosia* 'Fresh Look Gold', *Vinca* 'Pacifica Burgundy Halo', and *Petunia* 'Opera Supreme Pink Morn'. The closest All-America Selection display garden for Rhode Islanders is currently the one at the Massachusetts Horticultural Society's Elm Bank in Wellesley, but folks at the University of Rhode Island are working to create one on the university campus. Watch for it.

Right Annual, Right Place

While it can be great fun to buy an armload of annuals on a whim, it can be a strain on your wallet. It is perhaps more rewarding to know what you want and why before you make your purchase. Have a design plan in mind. Are you using the annuals for containers, to fill in spaces in a perennial bed, or for a cutting garden? Is your soil heavy clay as on Prudence Island or in Foster or sandy loam like that in Greene? Some annuals, like the heavy-blooming hybrids, want fairly rich, fertile soil, whereas others, like nasturtiums, prefer poor soil. Do your research! In general I find that as long as the soil has plenty of organic matter and a pH of 6 to 7, then I'll have success. Annuals that do well in poor soils include begonias, salvias, portulaca, brachyscome, and verbenas.

Climate is something of a factor when selecting annuals. For instance, northern areas like North Smithfield or Woonsocket have always done well with cold-tolerant annuals. "We're about 10 degrees cooler in summer up here," says Linda Proulx of Bottle Gentian Garden in Foster, "so things like pansies bloom longer."

Vines

I have to make a plug for annual vines. They are often overlooked in planting schemes, but they are such a pleasure to grow. Quickly sprouting up tepees, sprawling across fences, climbing up walls and over archways, they create a delightful effect in the garden quickly. Black-eyed Susan vine (*Thumbergia alata*), cardinal climber (*Ipmoea* x *multifida*), hyacinth bean (*Dolichos lablab*), sweet peas (*Lathyrus odoratus*), and starglory (*Mina lobata*) are satisfying additions to the garden. The shocking pink Brazilian jasmine (*Mandevilla*) is one of my favorites. A perennial in its native Brazil, it grows quickly and works well as an annual in Rhode Island. If you feel inclined, you can cut it back and overwinter it in a greenhouse.

Heat-tolerant hybrids—such as Supertunias, Surfinas, diascias, and alyssum—extend the bloom time of plants that once petered out in the heat of more southern portions of the state.

Selecting Plants at the Nursery

Your neighborhood garden center stocks plants that perform well locally. "What sells is what grows," says June Halliday of Chaves' Gardens & Florist in Middletown. "People see friends or neighbors having good luck with something, and through word of mouth certain annuals start to become more popular."

When you're in the garden center, don't be put off if plants are not in bloom. This probably means that the nursery has been diligent about pinching back to help the plants grow stronger roots and bush out. If they are in bloom, pinch off the flowers when you get the plants home, and you'll get many more blooms later, once the plant settles in. Avoid plants that look sickly—yellowed or spotted leaves or wilted, weak stems. Knock the plant gently out of its pot to check that the root system is healthy. The roots should be white, moist, and well distributed in the pot—circling roots mean the plant is pot bound. If you're not happy with the roots, don't buy the plant. An annual will be around only for one season. There's no point in bringing home a plant that needs months of coddling before it looks good.

Starting from Seed

Whether you sow seeds indoors or outside, your seed-starting date is determined by your area's last frost date. Working back from the last frost, calculate the number of weeks for seed germination and for the seedling to be strong and healthy enough to be planted outside. Take into consideration whether the plant is hardy, half hardy, or an annual/tender perennial. *Park's Success with Seeds* by Anne Reilly is a must-have book if you like growing plants from seed.

Seed annuals in flats or individual pots in a good soilless seed-starting mix. The mix should be thoroughly moistened but not soggy. You can use dampened peat pots, too.

Read the seed packet for germination instructions. Most seeds are sown at a depth equal to three times their diameter. Some seeds need darkness to germinate: Once the seeds are sown, cover the flats with a light-blocking material or put the flats in a warm, dark cupboard. Other seeds need light to germinate: Don't cover the seeds with the mix, just press the seeds in.

Most seeds need a growing condition that is moist and warm, so cover the flats with a plastic lid that holds in moisture and acts like a minigreenhouse. I put my flats on top of the refrigerator in the basement. Lift the lid regularly to check the seeds; vent the lid if the soil is too moist and remove the cover when plants sprout.

You need a good source of light to grow annuals indoors—a *very* sunny windowsill can work if you turn the flats every day. A fluorescent light setup is more reliable. Leave the lights on for twelve to eighteen hours a day. (You can buy a timer for this purpose.) Place the lights 6 to 12 inches above the seedlings and lift the lights as the plants grow. Water to keep the soil moist, not wet. Watering from the bottom is best because it doesn't disturb the seedlings.

If seedlings suffer from damping-off (a fungal disease that causes young plants to wilt or collapse), you may lose some but not necessarily all the plants. Damping-off travels quickly, but I saved a flat of basil by taking a clean knife and cutting out a chunk of soil with more than the affected seedlings and throwing the chunk away. I managed to stop the spread of the disease and thus retained a good basil crop.

Seedlings with their second set of true leaves can be transplanted into individual pots. I prefer peat pots because the entire pot can be planted and the pots decompose. Some plants, like nasturtiums and sweet peas, don't like to be disturbed or transplanted from a pot, so either plant the seed directly in the ground or in peat pots. When seedlings have four true leaves, you can spray them with a dilute liquid seaweed fertilizer.

Planting and Tending

Plants that have been grown indoors will need to go through the process of "hardening off" to prepare them for life outdoors. Put young plants outside for an hour or so the first day. Increase the amount of time each day until they've been outside all day and night. Then they can be planted. You can also harden off plants in

Containers

Annuals in containers give almost instant gratification. You can plant more closely than you would in a border. Since the plants will be in the container only for one season and use up only a 4- to 6-inch depth of soil, they will survive happily in close quarters. You can design and start your entire container indoors and put it outside when the weather is right. Just remember to harden off plants before doing so. You can also change plants easily as the seasons change.

a cold frame—control the temperature by lifting and closing the lids so the plants don't cook or freeze inside the cold frame.

The roots of annuals usually stay within the top 4 to 6 inches of soil. There are two schools of thought about preparing the soil for annuals. One school says dig deep and amend the soil with plenty of organic material because it will retain moisture and encourage roots to grow deeper. The other school says deep cultivation isn't necessary because annuals' roots are shallow and tilling soil deeply exposes lots of weed seeds. The latter tends to be my approach.

Some annuals can grow too tall or a bit leggy in the pot, but if they have adventitious roots (roots that grow out from the stem) you may be able to plant them deeper than normal—to the depths of their lowest leaves. Sunflowers can be planted this way, as can tomatoes.

Annuals need basic care once in the ground. Mulch to keep weeds at bay and retain moisture, water (preferably with soaker hoses), remove weeds before they go to seed, and spot fertilize with a liquid seaweed fertilizer if you see some plants struggling. While most annuals need a richer soil because they will only be producing blooms for one season, others (like nasturtium and cosmos) prefer a lean soil. Read the literature to find out what each annual needs. Ensure that heavier feeders have all the nutrients they require. Slow-release fertilizers are a good addition to an annual planting.

Most annuals do better with regular deadheading so the plant doesn't waste energy setting seed. And some will stop flowering once they develop seedpods. Pinching or cutting spent blooms not only stimulates the plant to put energy into new blooms but also makes it look nicer.

At the End of the Season

As first frost approaches, you can harvest and save seeds. Collecting seeds is enormously satisfying and great for the wallet. Harvest the seed when ripe, usually when the seedpod or capsule turns brown and dry. Cut the capsule off at its base and let it fall into a paper bag or envelope. Store the bag indoors through the winter in a cool, dry place. Label the bag with the plant name and the year the seed was collected. Most seeds are viable for two to five years.

Many annuals cheerfully reseed themselves, thus earning the name self-sowers. Love-in-a-mist (*Nigella*) for instance, will pop up everywhere in your garden, as will many annual poppies. This is great if you have a cottage-garden design. In a controlled design you may want to limit the number of self-sowers you introduce, or you will live with volunteers for a long time. I personally love it when I come across a *Nicotiana* or *Verbena bonariensis* in a surprising place. If I don't want it there, I remove it.

After frost there are two ways of handling annuals—pull out the dead plants or leave their roots in the ground. Pulling out the annuals leaves holes in the beds that can look unattractive and serve as homes for weed seeds unless you top-dress with compost or mulch with shredded leaves. Lift much of this mulch in the spring to help the soil warm up. If you leave the plants in the ground, their root systems will decompose over the winter. Cut the plants back to the ground so the garden looks neater.

Either way, clear away debris that could potentially harbor insects, pests, or diseases. Since annuals are only around for one season, there's not much time for them to become disease ridden, but some varieties can be susceptible to powdery mildew, rust, and gray mold. Bag and trash the leaves and stems of infected plants to avoid a repeat performance next year. Removing debris also makes it more difficult for insects such as aphids, leaf miners, spider mites, and whiteflies to overwinter. (Turn to chapter 10 for information on pests and diseases and how to control them.)

Great Annuals

In February it's always tempting to buy handfuls of seed packets of unusual annuals, but how often have you found yourself without the time or wherewithal to get all those seeds started? Fortunately, many local garden centers have started to sell quite unusual annuals as well as the "perennial" favorites. Let's look at some great annuals and their uses in Rhode Island gardens.

Easy Drama

Sarah Partyka owns the Farmer's Daughter in South Kingstown, a destination nursery for gardeners from Rhode Island and neighboring states. Partyka particularly likes the following annuals because they are "easy to grow and will give great results. Lots of bold foliage and different textures will add drama to your garden," she says.

Bush violet (*Browallia americana*). "A great little filler that is free-flowering all summer, with blue or white starlike flowers," Partyka says. Grows 1½ to 2 feet tall. Light shade to full sun.

Castor beans (*Ricinus*). Talk about dramatic—this plant's tropical foliage reaches 8 feet tall and has leaves large enough to act as umbrellas. The flowers develop into bright red, spiny seedpods. But note that the seedpods are poisonous! Full sun to part shade.

Flowering tobacco (*Nicotiana sylvestris*). This dramatic, tall white flowering plant releases its perfume in the evening.

"Hummingbirds and sphinx moths love them," Partyka says. Full sun to part shade.

Love-lies-bleeding (*Amaranthus erythrostachys*). Upright tassel-like flowers that are deep red, plus red foliage. It's a self-sower that will reach 10 feet in one season. Sun to part shade.

Mexican sunflower (*Tithonia rotundifolia*). "Large, bold, velvety leaves adorn 4-inch, bright orange daisylike flowers," Partyka notes. "This plant reaches 5 feet tall and loves the dog days of summer." Full sun.

Verbena bonariensis. This delightful weaver seeds itself everywhere. Erect stems support clusters of purple flowers. "No deadheading needed—and it is a butterfly magnet." Full sun to part shade.

Blithewold's Basics

When I worked alongside Gail Read, the horticulturist at Blithewold Mansion, Gardens & Arboretum in Bristol, she always claimed that she could never be without sweet peas, four o'clocks, poppies, nasturtiums, and old-fashioned *Heliotrope arborescens*. Read is known as the "Queen of Annuals." Here are some of her other favorites:

Basil (*Ocimum* 'African Blue'). "It blooms constantly without bolting, has a great structure and scent, and it attracts bees," Read says.

Fountain grass (*Pennisetum ruppelianum*). This grass offers graceful foliage with soft, bronze pink flower panicles in August. It has been a Blithewold favorite for almost two decades.

Marigolds. "I love single-flowering varieties 'LuLu', 'Signet Starfire', and 'Cottage Red'. 'Butter and Sugar' is a tall variety with small flowers."

Milkweed (*Asclepias physocarpus* 'Oscar'). "Seeds started in March zoom up to 6 feet by August," Read notes. "This one has little white flowers followed by green, hairy puffballs in September."

Morning glory (*Ipomoea* 'Heavenly Blue'). "A sentimental favorite," she says. "It's a classic with a great blue color."

Tassel flower (*Emilia javanica*). "Both the orange and scarlet varieties flower constantly but need frequent deadheading. Massed plantings are eye catching even though the flowers are small."

Zinnias, Profusion series: 'Apricot' and 'Fire'. "Very mildew resistant and constantly blooming—and the blooms last for a long time."

A Tropical Rhode Island!

Tropical plants In Rhode Island? No way! you say. But Hall-of-Fame URI CE Master Gardener Elaine Powers grows them in East Greenwich, and not just as house plants. She admits they require additional work, but "that is the love of gardening for me," she says. Powers plants tropicals every year, enjoys them through the summer, and then digs them up in the fall for storage.

Landscape designer Louis Raymond, principal of Hopkinton-based Renaissance Gardening, has created a reputation based on his flamboyant designs and unusual choices of plant material. Here are a few tropicals that Raymond likes to use as annuals in his designs:

Apricot fuchsia (*Fuchsia* 'Gartenmeister Bonstedt'). "Blooms continuously, even through a sweltering August," Raymond reports. "Clusters of narrow apricot trumpets dance over contrasting purple leaves."

Brazilian glory bush (*Thouchina semidecandra*). This South American bush has green, fuzzy leaves and large, loose clusters of red buds that open into iridescent indigo five-petaled blossoms.

Canna lilies (*Canna* spp.). "Banana-like foliage but without the banana's trunklike stems. Both leaves and flowers can be had in adventurous and even raucous melees of pink, yellow, orange, pink, cream, and green—sometimes all on the same plant!"

Elephant's ears (*Alocasia*). This huge tribe of plants offers triangular leaves even bigger than those of the banana. It's all about the foliage, which can be purple, shiny green, acid chartreuse, or green-white variegated.

New Zealand flax (*Phormium tenax*). "Looking like fancy-leaved iris on steroids, there are dozens of *Phormium* cultivars with sword-shaped leaves in various combinations of purple, green, yellow, white, or even pink stripes," Raymond says. "No flowers in Rhode Island, but with this foliage, who cares!"

Ornamental bananas (*Ensete* spp.). "With rich soil, heat, sun, and plenty of water, even small starter sizes can morph into monsters by September," he says. "Enormous paddle-shaped leaves atop a tall trunklike stem are a dramatic contrast to hardy plants. Best in my book is the purple-flushed variety, *E. maurelii*, the red Abyssinian banana."

Red bird-of-paradise (*Caesalpinia pulcherrima*). Lacy blue green foliage is topped with heads of glowing orange red flowers. Butterflies and hummingbirds will be ecstatic!

Tara ginger (*Hedychium densiflorum* 'Tara'). Strong vertical canes grow from vigorous rhizomes, topped in late summer by large spikes of fragrant flowers in white, yellow, or orange.

Variegated parlor maple (*Abutilon* 'Souvenir de Bonn'). Grow this for the foliage: large maplelike leaves with a wide white border. The bell-shaped orange flowers at the tips of each branch are lovely but not essential.

Annuals are particularly enjoyable to grow with children. Because annuals fill out so quickly, it's fun to take youngsters out into the garden to see their plants thriving. And for the grown-up, nothing beats wandering around the garden just before dinner doing a little stress-releasing deadheading or gathering flowers to go on the table. You can pick as many blossoms as you want, because cutting only encourages more flowers. The constant supply of blooms and the speed with which annuals grow make them indispensable in the garden.

CHAPTER FIVE

Perennials

As a novice gardener I thought "perennial" was synonymous with easy. Not so! Growing perennials is more of a challenge than I anticipated—fun, but still a challenge. A perennial, once established, can survive for five or more years, but not without care or help.

Rhode Island gardeners contend with varied weather patterns every year, so getting our plants to perform the way we want is tricky. Some years spring warmth arrives in April. Other years we experience true springlike weather for only two weeks in May, followed immediately by hot summer temperatures and dry spells. In 2006 the extended warm fall weather caused my cherry tree (*Prunus subhirtella* 'Autumnalis') to bloom on Christmas Day! Even the experts aren't sure what to do in a climate that's so unpredictable. But selecting the right perennials, putting them in the right place, and giving them the care they need is a good start.

Perennials 101

First, some definitions. A perennial is a plant that comes back year after year. It produces flowers and seeds more than once in its life span. When people think of perennials, what usually comes to mind are the standard herbaceous perennials like astilbe, bee balm, daylily, and iris. But perennials also include cacti, succulents, wildflowers, ferns, grasses, bamboos, and roses.

Perennials can be herbaceous or woody.

Herbaceous perennials are those with soft stems. The top—stems, leaves, and flowers— usually die to the ground each fall. The parts of the plant that are underground survive the winter. Bleeding heart (*Dicentra*) is a herbaceous perennial.

Woody perennials are often referred to as subshrubs. Their stems are woody and stiff. A woody perennial does not die back to its crown or roots as does a herbaceous perennial, and so it generally is not cut back in fall. Woody perennials like Russian sage (*Perovskia*) are often pruned like a shrub.

Roses

In my view roses are in a category all their own. They are closer in habit to a woody perennial. I love roses, but I can't do them justice in the space of this book. I suggest contacting the American Rose Society at www.ars.org (their book, *The Rose*, is a helpful guide) and the Rhode Island Rose Society at www.rirs.org for rose-growing information specific to our region. There are numerous books on roses, but keep your ear to the ground for a new book by Rhode Islanders Mike and Angelina Chute, both American Rose Society certified consulting rosarians. Their book will focus exclusively on roses for New England. The May/June 2007 issue of *People, Places & Plants* magazine featured a Q&A on growing roses in New England written by the Chutes.

To see rose displays in Rhode Island, visit Blithewold Mansion, Gardens & Arboretum in Bristol, the Victorian Rose Garden in Roger Williams Park in Providence, the new Roger Williams Park Botanical Center, and the Chet Clayton Sustainable Rose Garden at the University of Rhode Island Botanical Gardens (see chapter 12 for contact information).

Hardiness Zones and Perennials

Hardiness zone ratings are important when selecting perennials. Perennials fall into three categories based on their reaction to cold.

Hardy perennials can survive Rhode Island winters without protection, or with very little protection.

Half-hardy or **semihardy perennials** need some protection (such as mulch) from winter cold.

Tender perennials, which are often tubers, bulbs, or rhizomes, won't survive Rhode Island winters. They need to be lifted in fall, stored through the winter, and replanted the following spring when the soil warms. A few that fall into that category are *Agastache* 'Summerbreeze', *Cuphea* 'David Verity', *Stachytarpheta jamaicensis* 'Coral Form', and *Senecio veravera*. See chapter 4 for more on using tender perennials as annuals.

Hardy perennials such as bellflower (*Campanula*), coneflower (*Echinacea*), and columbine (*Aquilegia*) can handle colder temperatures and therefore are rated for a different hardiness zone than

The Perennial Plant of the Year

The Perennial Plant Association (www.perennialplant.org) is a trade association that selects and promotes one plant each year. "The Perennial Plant of the Year program helps consumers select plants that perennial industry experts find to be outstanding and easily grown," says executive director Steven Still. You can see the featured plants on the Web site or find selections suitable for a range of climate types, low maintenance, easy propagation, and multiple-season interest. Recent selections have included *Nepeta* 'Walkers Low' (2007), *Dianthus gratianopolitanus* 'Firewitch' (2006), *Helleborus* x *hybridus* (2005), and *Athyrium niponicum* 'Pictum' (2004).

tender perennials like a lot of the salvias, dahlias, or coleus. Remember, however, that your USDA Hardiness Zone rating (see chapter 2) is only a guideline. There is never a guarantee that a plant will survive in your garden, even if the experts say it will. Planting for your conditions is the best advice I can give.

Designing with Perennials

Most perennials do not bloom all summer. This makes designing with perennials a sometimes-exciting challenge. I don't particularly mind if my plants are not in bloom all the time because I have a soft spot for foliage color and texture. But if you want constant flower color in your garden, design your garden for a constant succession of bloom. Learn the bloom time of each perennial and choose plants that flower at different times in the spring, summer, and fall. By artfully staggering the plants' locations through the border, you lead the eye from bloom to bloom all season long.

You can have fun by planning gardens with different color themes in different months. Or you may want the look of a monochromatic garden, like the famous all-white garden at Sissinghurst in England. You can design with just one plant like daylilies, irises, or hostas— all of which have varieties with slightly different bloom times. You can design a mixed border that is predominantly perennials but that is offset by the structure of shrubs and filled in with constantly blooming annuals. Shrubs like hydrangea, butterfly bush (*Buddleia*), and deutszia work well in these designs.

You may want a garden that peaks in spring or a garden designed specifically for the fall. Your choices may depend on where you spend your time at different times of the year. My spring garden is in the front of our house, where I can see it from the front room. The summer and fall gardens and the cutting garden are at the back of the house so we can view them from the kitchen and deck, where we spend the warm weather.

Louis Raymond, principal of Renaissance Gardening in Hopkinton, designs with plants that are "engaging and different" and always dramatic. He looks for perennials that:

- Don't need excessive intervention with staking or dividing or pest fighting or winter protection.

- Establish in a season or two.

- Don't "burst out of the gate in spring full of excitement but collapse by July after they're done blooming."

- Are interesting to look at even when not in flower, so they must have great foliage.

- Are flexible about being moved or divided.

- Won't be a "self-disaster" if you forget to deadhead.

- Are collegial citizens, not invading into all the neighboring plants.

- Are a bit out of the norm, so that you don't grow the same plants that all your neighbors own.

With those criteria in mind, Raymond says "these truly are champs": leopard plant (*Ligularia japonica*), rosinweed (*Silphium perfoliatum*), *Iris ensata* 'Variegata', toad lily (*Tricyrtis hirta* 'Alba'), spiderwort (*Tradescantia* 'Sweet Kate'), monkshood (*Aconitum henryi* 'Sparks'), and cranesbill (*Geranium macrorrhizum* 'Czakor').

Barbara's Border for Constant Color

I designed these herbaceous perennials into a Zone 6a border for a succession of bloom. They all require sun to light shade.

Plant	Bloom Time	Color
Daffodil (*Narcissus*)	April–May	Yellow
Candytuft (*Iberis sempervirens*)	April–June	White
Bleeding heart (*Dicentra spectabilis*)	April–June	Deep pink
Lady's mantle (*Alchemilla mollis*)	May–June	Chartreuse and green
Ornamental onion (*Allium aflatunense*)	May–June	Purple
Cornflower (*Centaurea*)	May–July	Blue
Catnip (*Nepeta mussini*)	May–October	Lavender and gray
Meadow sage (*Salvia x superba*)	May–October	Blue
Queen-of-the-prairie (*Filipendula rubra*)	July–September	Lavender
Snakeroot (*Eupatorium rugosum*)	August–October	White

Sun or Shade?

Some books say that the best site for a perennial border is in full sun—that is, six to eight hours of sun per day. I think that limits your choices: There are so many perennials that like the shade or partial shade. My favorite border is in the shade. My girls dubbed it "Shady Glade." It's not quite that glamorous, but it contains some gorgeous bugbane (*Cimicifuga*), hostas, hellebores, ginger, ferns, rodgersia, and more.

There are wonderful shade displays at the University of Rhode Island Botanical Gardens, at Blithewold, and at some garden centers like the Potting Shed in Portsmouth and the Farmer's Daughter in South Kingstown. Or read books on shade-loving perennials, like Ken Druse's *The Natural Shade Garden*. You'll see why I like shade.

Borders or Islands?

Most gardening books, English or American, show perennial borders against some sort of backdrop—a hedge, fence, or shrubs—because that was how borders were traditionally placed. That is, until Alan Bloom of Bressingham's in England decided to bring a perennial border out into the middle of the garden as an "island bed."

Whether a single border set against a backdrop, or a double border with a walkway between, traditional beds are usually designed to be seen from only one side—the front. The island bed is meant to be seen from every angle, which is trickier to design. Traditional one-sided borders usually have taller plants at the back, gradating down in size to the low, mounding plants at the front. The edges can be crisp, straight, and formal or soft and undulating with plants like catnip (*Nepeta*), lady's mantle (*Alchemilla mollis*), or low-growing candytuft (*Iberis*) flopping over the edge for a softer effect. Sometimes a garden structure, such as a tepee with climbing plants, can establish the focal point for height, particularly in an island bed.

Whether you choose a border or an island bed, cluster your plants in groups of three or five and carry the groups through the border so your bed is more than a collection of "one of everything." Groupings draw the eye along the border. Plant form, structure, and foliage are just as important as flower color. Each plant should be interesting to look at after its blooms have passed. When using plants like ornamental onion (*Allium*), where the foliage dies back even while the plant is in bloom, then be sure that another plant (like hosta) comes fast behind to mask the spent foliage. Consider using a tall, transparent plant, such as *Verbena bonariensis*, occasionally in the front. Transparent plants create a veil through which one sees the rest of the border—they give height and color without blocking the view.

Designing with perennials is often about mixing in other plants. Anne Wilson has maintained a garden at a private estate in Newport for many years and regularly mixes shrubs and annuals into her perennial borders. For annuals, cleome is a must, along with white browallia and New Guinea impatiens. Her choice of perennials? "I use lady's mantle everywhere," she says, "and iris, meadow rue (*Thalictrum*), bugbane, toad lily (*Trycirtis*), hostas of any sort, different hydrangeas, and the old standbys: *Hakonechloa, Houttuynia,* ginger, variegated Solomon's seal."

Containers

Perennials can be grown in containers for the deck or front porch, but in most places in Rhode Island you would need to bring the containers into the house or a greenhouse to overwinter the plants, if you have room. Container perennials should have strong foliage or structural interest because the blooms won't last. Bergenia, for example, looks super in a container—its architectural leaves and red stems look good even when its pink flowers have gone by.

Acquiring Perennials

Note that I write "acquiring" and not "buying." Perennials often grow to such a size that they need to be divided, and that's when gardeners start looking to give away divisions. Pass-along plants are great if the plant is something you want. But "buyer beware"—this generosity may not always work in your favor. Maybe the plant is too vigorous, and in two years' time you, too, will have to divide and dispose of it. Make sure you know the characteristics of what you're being offered. And acquaint yourself with the state list of invasive plants (see chapter 9) so that you don't introduce offenders to your garden.

Other ways to acquire perennials are by propagating them (easiest from cuttings), growing them from seed, and purchasing.

Buy from a reputable nursery, know what you're looking for by the foliage, and trust the label. (Chances are the perennial will not be in bloom when you locate it.) Look closely at the foliage to ensure the plant is healthy. Yellowed, shriveled, spotted, or insect-damaged leaves are signs of problems. Leave those plants behind. Tap a plant out of its pot to make sure the roots are healthy.

Perennial Care

The roots of perennials often grow deep. In the case of peonies, for instance, the roots extend down as much as 2 feet. You can constantly improve and amend the soil in an annual or vegetable bed, but it's hard to make changes or improvements to an established perennial bed without disturbing what's already growing there.

For that reason, prepare the perennial bed deeply and thoroughly at the outset. Adjust the soil pH and add organic amendments as necessary to improve the soil tilth, texture, and condition (refer to chapter 1). Perennials won't like being constantly disturbed once they are established. Fall is a good time to prepare a new perennial bed. This gives the organic material and microbes time to settle in and do their work before you plant in the spring.

Pay attention to the size the plant will become. It's tempting to build a new perennial bed by thickly planting perennials so that the bed looks immediately finished. I know because I've done it. New plants look small. It's hard to believe that something in a gallon container will grow to be the size of a small shrub in two years. Resist the temptation to plant too closely—fill in with annuals if you don't like the sparse look of a newly installed border.

Before putting plants into the ground, water each perennial well in its pot, ideally the day before planting. Dig a hole that accommodates the full spread of the plant's roots: Remember the adage "a hundred-dollar hole for a ten-dollar plant." Sprinkle in a little slow-release organic fertilizer to give the plant a nutrient boost. Plant the crown of the plant at soil level—which may not be the way the plant currently sits in the nursery pot. Then water the plant in. Keep the soil moist for the first week or two, after which you can ease off and establish a regular watering routine (see chapter 3). You may want to cut or pinch back a plant with heavy top growth so that its energy goes into the roots rather than the foliage. Perennials don't always look fabulous when they're first planted. They look better the second year and come into their own from year three onward.

Transplanting

In general the best time to transplant a perennial, whether spring blooming or fall blooming, is after it has finished flowering. But some late fall-blooming perennials, like boltonia, may prefer to be transplanted in the spring. Shallow-rooted perennials. like heuchera or astilbe, may also prefer to be transplanted in the spring because they are prone to cold heaving them out of the soil if planted too late in the year. They need time to establish a good base before the freeze of winter hits. You can transplant in the middle of summer, but you will have to pamper the plant with extra care and water. It will have a tougher time establishing itself unless well cared for. Certain plants (like irises) go dormant after they have bloomed and can be divided at that time—usually late spring or early summer.

I tend to think that if the plant is unaware that it's being moved, it will settle in quickly no matter when I move it. I dig up more soil around the plant than is really necessary so that I disturb its roots as little as possible, and I always have the receiving hole ready. When I slide the plant into the new hole, I don't think the plant is even aware that it's been moved.

Keep records of what you planted when and where. I can't tell you the number of times I've dug up my lovely white 'Thalia' daffodils in the fall because I've gone to plant something right where the daffodils are slumbering.

Perennials for All Places

No matter what your hardiness zone, there are remarkable perennials just right for your Rhode Island garden. Here are recommendations from the experts.

Waterside Wonders

The North Garden at Blithewold Mansion, Gardens & Arboretum in Bristol is a painter's palette of perennials that do well in Rhode Island and particularly in conditions close to water—in this case, the Narragansett Bay. Horticulturist Kristin Green reveals some favorite North Garden perennials:

Amsonia hubrectii. "Delicate midgreen willow leaves, topped by fleeting cerulean flowers in spring, turn entirely brilliant golden yellow in autumn," Green says.

Aster x *frikartii* '**Monch**'. Loose clusters of 2-inch French blue, yellow-centered daisies bloom from August into September.

Bellflower (*Campanula lactiflora* 'White Flower Farm

Selection'). Tall, pale, green leafy stalks are topped by branched clusters of sky blue, smallish open bells from June through July.

Catmint (*Nepeta* x *faassenii*). "A ground-grazing, kitten-soft, silver green and lavender cushion with an indescribable spicy-mint fragrance."

Clematis (*Clematis integrifolia*). This nonvining clematis has delicate, narrow, twisty petaled dark purple-blue flowers in July, followed by Phyllis Diller seed heads. It can be coaxed upright through a small peony ring, she says.

Cranesbill (*Geranium* 'Rozanne'). "Pinky purple blue-haloed saucer flowers don't know when to quit!" Green notes. This cultivar "blooms spring to frost and weaves among its front-row neighbors with loosely threaded pale to green foliage."

False indigo (*Baptisia australis*). Heavy, blue green pea foliage (great for arrangements) shoots to 3 feet by June, with stalks bearing momentary racemes of deep blue pea flowers.

Japanese anemone (*Anemone* x *hybrida* 'Andrea Atkinson'). White saucer flowers rise 3 to 4 feet out of clumps of dark green, buttercuplike foliage. 'Andrea Atkinson' starts blooming "early" for a Japanese anemone, in mid-August.

Lady's mantle (*Alchemilla mollis*). "Foaming clusters of tiny chartreuse flowers flop from late May into June out of clumps of sage green moleskin leaves," Green says.

Veronica (*Veronica longifolia*). Deep blue spikes on 4-foot stems of deep green leaves punctuate the back of the border through July into August.

Tough Plants for Sunny, Well-Drained Sites

Barbara Chaves co-owns Chaves' Gardens & Florist in Middletown with her brothers, Joe and Ron. At work she focuses on the florist division, but when tending her own garden at home she chooses plants that adapt to sunny, well-drained sites. "My yard is mostly sun or part sun with sandy loam," she says. "I'm so busy at work that my plants have to be able to endure tough love, but they must look good through most of the season whether they are in bloom or not!" Most of her selections have waxy coatings, furry leaves, or thick, fleshy leaves that can retain moisture in drought conditions. These same plants would do well by the coast, since similar conditions apply.

Bear's britches (*Acanthus spinosus*). "This has to be one of my favorite plants. The foliage is glossy and deeply divided. A handsome plant even when not in bloom, but then the show begins when numerous spikes of purple and gray shoot up from the center. Wow!"

Calamint (*Calamintha nepeta*). "The aromatic foliage is gray green and the tiny numerous flowers are white. Terrific in front of a stone wall."

Catmint (*Nepeta* 'Walker's Low'). "I like a lot of nepetas, but this is a favorite. Looks good, smells good, and is easy to grow. Cut back after blooming and it starts over again."

Gas plant (*Dictamnus albus*). "This shoots up in spring and makes a statement when everything else is feeling pokey," she explains. It has lupinelike flowers in the early spring, and later it develops interesting seedpods.

Joe-pye weed (*Eupatorium purpureum*). "I love all varieties, but this has the distinction of purple foliage."

Lamb's ears (*Stachys bysantina*). "I would not be without this. Its low, silvery foliage is the right companion for just about any plant."

Penstemon 'Husker Red'. "I enjoy the foliage more than the plant. A great upright, burgundy beauty."

Phlox 'Bright Eyes'. "Who can be without this? I have never had powdery mildew on it."

"These are my favorites because they are hardy and dependable," she says. "The more chic plants fill in around them!"

Favorites from a Must-See Garden

As a longtime gardener and member of the Rhode Island

Federation of Garden Clubs, Niamh Maddock's Barrington garden is often on display on garden tours. I can't tell you how many people have said, "You *must* see Niamh Maddock's garden!" Maddock graciously shares a selection of her favorite perennials:

Chrysanthemum x *suberbum* 'Becky' was the 2003 perennial of the year, "and justly so," Maddock says. "It is a wonderful plant that is easily divided, and blooms forever if deadheaded. Like phlox, it is a structural plant and needs space or it will overrun its neighbors."

Corydalis 'Blue Panda' and *Brunnera macrophylla* 'Jack Frost'. "I mention these together because they are a spectacular combination. I had both plants in a holding area some years ago when I noticed that the flowers were exactly the same shade of forget-me-not blue. It is a hard color to match at any time, being a true blue without any violet cast to it."

Crambe cordifolia. "This is a sulky, bad-tempered plant that would rather produce foliage than flowers. If you can persuade it to behave, it will become a 6-footer that looks like *Gypsophila* (baby's breath) on steroids," Maddock explains.

Hellebores. "The runaway winners of early spring have to be the hellebores. There are two main kinds available here, *Helleborus niger* and *H. orientalis*, otherwise known as the Christmas rose and the Lenten rose. The Christmas roses are all white. The Lenten roses come in a variety of pink and purple and have freckled faces. Both varieties turn pale green with age, rather like hydrangeas."

Rockcress (white *Arabis*). "This very early gray-leaf ground cover starts blooming in March. Mine continues until well into June and is top of my list of good investment plants. It hangs about on the top of stonewalls and at the dry edge of patio and terrace beds. It will rot in damp or fertilized soil; it thrives on sun, drought, and neglect."

Shooting star (*Dodecatheon*). This spring-flowering plant's "delicacy of form is positively addictive," Maddock says.

"*Dodecatheon* belongs to the primrose family; it is a small plant with an 8- or 9-inch slender stem that holds a terminal umbel of nodding white flowers."

Wood lilies. "*Trillium erectum* is a large trillium that shows off a burgundy flower and a huge circular leaf for many weeks in spring. *T. grandiflorum* is actually a small plant and qualifies as a spring ephemeral, as the foliage vanishes pretty quickly after the flower degrades. The white flower turns a slightly mottled pink as it ages and is very attractive for quite a long time. There is a truly magical double form of the plant called *Trillium* 'Flore Pleno', which takes years to establish and costs a king's ransom."

Perennial Maintenance

Weeds compete for everything—nutrients, water, air, space. Get rid of them! Simple as that. We used to be taught to cultivate the soil vigorously—always. But vigorous cultivation may destroy soil texture, bring weed seeds to the surface, or snap off weeds so that their roots remain in the soil and multiply. I'm still dealing with chickweed that in my younger gardening days I did not remove correctly (see chapter 10 for details of proper weed treatment). The best approach is to loosen the soil simply by inserting a fork in the soil between plants and gently moving the fork back and forth. This motion opens up the soil and makes it easier to uproot weeds, and it doesn't overly disturb what's growing.

Depending on weather, your perennials may need regular watering. Then there's the deadheading, pinching, debudding, pruning, staking, and cutting back. These all make the plant look nicer and help it put energy into root growth and new bushy upper growth.

Should you cut back top growth in autumn? A late-fall cleanup of herbaceous perennials has benefits—it tidies the garden and cuts down on chores in the spring. But leaving some stems up through winter gives the garden visual definition and provides food and protection for wildlife. I like to see the seed heads of coneflower (*Echinacea*), Jerusalem artichoke (*Helianthus tuberosus*), and black-eyed Susan (*Rudbeckia*). I'm prepared for the extra work in the spring—it's a tradeoff.

Woody perennials like Russian sage (*Perovskia*), catmint (*Nepeta*), or lavender (*Lavandula*) do not respond well to being cut back in the fall. They may even die. Woody perennials are best pruned of deadwood in spring once you see a substantial flush of new growth.

Part of garden maintenance is keeping an eye out for problems caused by pests and diseases. You can minimize problems by keeping plants healthy, planting them in the right conditions, and treating them well.

Watching for life in your perennial bed in the spring is one of life's particular pleasures. The energy is palpable. Yes, there are bittersweet moments. Perhaps your favorite anemone didn't make it through the winter. But then you look to your right and see last year's new cranesbill starting to show through—and you smile. Perennials are the Energizer Bunny of gardening—they just keep on going.

Vegetable Gardening

I seem to know a lot of good vegetable gardeners in Rhode Island. Maybe it's the old-time farmer in them. As I look out at my husband tending his tomatoes, I see how satisfying growing veggies can be. It looks easy—deceptively easy! But I don't recommend winging it with vegetables—you'll waste time and resources and may end up with a scrappy crop. Before you even put vegetable seed into soil, think about your gardening goals. You need a plan.

The good news is even if you're short on time or space, you can still grow vegetables. You can incorporate them into your flower and shrub borders or grow them in containers. You can have any size vegetable garden. Voracious gardener Dick Elliott, who lives around the corner from me in Portsmouth, has a tiny vegetable garden—two 10-by-4-foot beds raised 4 feet high to make tending them easier on his back, and all enclosed with a little picket fence. It's exactly what he needs, and it is a showpiece.

Location, Location, Location

At the outset, decide where to locate the vegetable garden. Most vegetables need six to eight hours of sunlight a day and prefer eight to ten hours. Fruiting vegetables like tomatoes, peppers, or squash need a full day of sun. Root vegetables like carrots or beets can tolerate less, and leafy vegetables like lettuce can handle quite a lot of shade.

South-facing beds are optimum. A slight slope is good. If you have steep slopes, consider terracing. Don't locate the garden at the bottom of a hill where cold air and water collects.

For ease of harvesting, situate a vegetable garden near the kitchen. Locate the garden near a source of water, such as a spigot, or bring a hose outlet extension to the garden. Install rain barrels to collect extra rainfall (see chapter 3).

If your site is windy, protect your crops. The wind can dry out

Support Your Local Farmer

Can't grow your own produce? Consider purchasing your vegetables through a farm that participates in Community Supported Agriculture. Here's how CSA works: You pay a fee to become a member, and by so doing you make a commitment to help support a local farm through the season. You pay for your vegetables at the beginning of the season. This money helps the farmer to grow the produce. You then go to the farm every week to pick up your share of what has been harvested. It's great fun and very social—you meet like-minded people, you help support vegetable farming, and you get great vegetables. What could be better?

To find a CSA participating farm near you, log on to Farm Fresh Rhode Island's expansive Web site at www.farmfreshri.org. The nonprofit FFRI lists each farm in Rhode Island and describes the type kind of farm, if the farm is organic, and what vegetables or fruits it grows. The Web site also lists farmers' markets, farm stands, nutrition, and more. Or you can get information from the Rhode Island Department of Environmental Management Web site at www.dem.ri.gov.

Rhode Island's Giant Pumpkins

Rhode Island has become the worldwide hotbed of giant pumpkin growing, says Danny Dill of Howard Dill Enterprises in Nova Scotia, which supplies most of the competition-level seeds. His father, Howard Dill, originated the 'Atlantic Giant', from which many of these behemoths have sprouted. "The best giant pumpkin growers in the world are in Rhode Island," asserts Ron Wallace of Greene, who broke the world record in October 2006 with his 1,502-pound pumpkin. The annual Rhode Island Southern New England Giant Pumpkin Growers Championship—known locally only as "the weigh-off"—is held every October at Frerich's Farm in Warren (www.frerichsfarm.com).

Who would think the smallest state could generate the world's biggest pumpkin! Contact the Southern New England Giant Pumpkin Growers Association at (401) 864-7747 for more information.

or batter them. Build protection in the form of built structures or shrubs, keeping these protective elements at a height that won't reduce available sunlight, and make them permeable to let air through.

The best soil for vegetables is deep, moist, and friable, with abundant organic material and microbial life. Different crops like a slightly different pH, and you may need to adjust soil accordingly (see chapter 1). Well-draining soil is important. Vegetables don't like wet feet and tend to develop root rot and fungal diseases if kept too damp. If you have poorly draining soil, consider building raised beds for better drainage.

"There aren't many vegetables we can't grow here," notes David Frerich of Frerich's Farm in Warren. "We have so many types of soil in Rhode Island. Even the long-day vegetables will grow well if you give them a head start in your house or greenhouse."

Vegetable Garden Design

The size of your vegetable garden will be dictated by a number of factors, the first being the size of the site. If you have only 3 square feet of yard in full sun, that's the size of your garden—unless you're able to remove nearby trees or fences to open up a larger area. Next, consider your work and family schedule: How much time you have to devote to the garden? Finally, evaluate what you plan to grow in the garden. If you want only lettuce, tomatoes, and a few herbs, then you won't need a huge bed—you could get by with containers. But if you plan to incorporate four compost areas, a greenhouse, corn, asparagus, squash, and an assortment of climbing vegetables, then you will need a lot of space.

For the most part vegetable gardening is annual gardening, but there are a few perennial vegetables, such as rhubarb or asparagus. Plan your gardens so that perennial vegetables are together in one area and you'll find maintenance becomes easier. At the end of the season, you cut back your perennials in their spot and completely empty out the rest of the beds. In the spring you don't have to pick your way through the perennials randomly located through the garden; you simply start all over again with the new veggie annuals in the open areas.

You can design your vegetable garden in any configuration: straight rows, square beds, circles—or a combination of these. The primary concern is to give your plants the right amount of space to thrive. Research each vegetable variety's recommended spacing, measured from the center of one plant to the center of another. You want the garden to be efficient. You want to be able to reach your vegetables without clambering around the garden, compacting the soil and damaging your soaker hoses. And you want chores like weeding to be as easy as possible. But have fun—it's *your* garden.

Contained raised beds can be built to a variety of levels—even waist high. Soil drains well in raised beds, warms up more quickly in spring, and retains warmth longer in fall. It's easy to reach weeds and harvest vegetables. Raised beds also look neat, clean, and efficient.

Uncontained mounded rows are easy to create. Spread a thick layer of newspapers on the ground, top with a layer of humus-rich soil, and then plant. Mounded rows offer similar benefits to raised beds, though they don't look quite as neat. Water drains well from the beds but care is needed when watering because water may collect in the pathways, and runoff may lead to soil erosion.

Sunken trenches hold water and therefore may not drain well. They are also are hard work to create.

I like to experiment, so I have tried most of these designs. I like waist-high raised beds because they are easy on the back.

What to Grow

Grow what you want to eat and only enough for your family and friends. It sounds obvious, but it's easy to get carried away when the catalogs arrive in winter. Before you know it, you've ordered all sorts of vegetables that your family won't touch.

Probably the most important things to consider when growing vegetables in Rhode Island are temperature ranges and frost dates, which dictate the length of the growing season. Jayne Merner Senecal in Charlestown has had many frosts well into May. "I recommend that all gardeners wait until at least Memorial Day to plant tender plants like basil and tomatoes outside. Our farm sits at the bottom of a hill where frost settles. Even when no other farms get hit, we do. I don't plant our tender annuals until June 1."

URI Cooperative Extension Master Gardener Paula Mottshaw, up in Foster, has a short growing season. "I don't do much direct seeding," she says, "with the exception of root crops (carrots, parsnips, rutabagas, turnips, beets) and beans. Everything else I grow in our small 8-by-10-foot unheated greenhouse." For heat-loving crops like peppers, tomatoes, melons, and eggplant, Mottshaw covers the soil with black plastic for about two weeks before planting to warm the soil. In the fall she uses row covers to extend the season.

Crops that do best when planted from mid-July to mid-August are short-season, early varieties that tolerate cooler nights and shorter days.

Veggie Ideas

If you're trying to decide what to plant in your garden, consider the kinds of veggies grown successfully at Rhode Island farms.

For example, Skip Paul and his wife, Liz Peckham, have been farming organically at Wishing Stone Farm for more than twenty-eight years. "Our soils in Little Compton lack good drainage, but on the other hand they have many secondary nutrients in abundance, which is why we grow potatoes and brassicas like broccoli, cabbage, and cauliflower so well." Unusual vegetables that grow well at the farm are artichokes, oyster plant, celariac, diakon, raddichio, pole beans, Chinese long beans, Egyptian zucchini, Romanesco cauliflower, and purple and orange cauliflower. About the only vegetable they struggle with is celery.

With the advent of new technologies like "walk-in tunnels," Paul and Peckham can grow just about anything they set their minds to. "Next year with walk-in tunnels we will be growing our first orchard of fig trees!" he says. "People at the farmers' markets will die for a real tree-ripened fresh fig."

At Frerich's Farm in Warren, the site of the world-famous giant pumpkin weigh-off, David and Barbara Frerich grow 2,000 varieties of annuals, perennials, herbs, and vegetables. "Honeydews, cantaloupes, and watermelons are easy to grow with a little boost from the greenhouse. Okra is another one that does surprisingly well up north," says David Frerich. "As long as your soil isn't too hard, the root crops will do well for you." He particularly likes heirloom varieties of tomatoes. "I love 'Cherokee Purple' even though the disease resistance isn't high. It may be a strange color, but it sure tastes good. 'Juliet' is a small plum/grape variety that has a fabulous flavor."

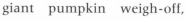

Over on the west passage of Narragansett Bay is Casey Farm, a 300-acre historic working farm owned by Historic New England (www.historicnewengland.org). The farm staff raise vegetables, small fruit, flowers, and poultry for a 200-member Community Supported Agriculture program and for two local farmers' markets. Mike Hutchison, farm manager, offers a taste of what grows well on the windy site:

- 'Athena' cantaloupe. A large, sweet, late-season melon. Tastes best in a hot, dry year.

- 'Bright Lights' Swiss chard. "A beautiful variety of chard that comes in an array of colors. Healthy and prolific," Hutchison says.

- 'Everhardy' garlic. Large bulbs form at the base of 2- to 3-foot stalks, with three to four large cloves per bulb.

- 'Fairy Tale' eggplants. "Small (3 to 4 inches) purple and white splashed fruit make for great grilling," Hutchison says.

- 'Hakarei' turnip. "A small, white, sweet turnip best grown in the spring and fall. Best eaten raw and in salads," he advises.

- 'Nelson' carrots. An early sweet carrot with abundant spring production.

- 'Persimmon' tomato. A large orange slicing tomato great for sandwiches; supersweet.

- 'Red Long of Tropea' onions. An excellent early-season elongated red salad onion.

- 'Tender Sweet' cabbage. "Small headed and sweet. A great backyard cabbage."

- 'Zepher' summer squash. A prolific yellow straightneck squash with a green tip.

"Odd veggies that work well for us in coastal Rhode Island" include 'Imperial Star' artichokes, a variety developed as an annual for cooler climates; 'Georgia Jet' sweet potatoes, a short season variety that is very prolific; 'Burgundy Red' okra, which does well along the coast; bulb fennel; green soybeans; and celeriac, a long-season crop grown for its softball-size root used in soups and salads. "We buy most of our seeds from Johnny's Seeds in Maine," Hutchison notes, "but also pick up a few things from Fedco Seeds, Germainia, Totally Tomatoes, Seed Savers Exchange, and a few others."

Valuable Vegetable Resources

The College of the Environment and Life Sciences at URI is a dynamic educational institution for both students and the public. Their Web site www.uri.edu/cels is just chock-full of great information on growing vegetables. Rudi Hempe is a Hall-of-Fame URI Cooperative Extension Master Gardener and retired newspaper man who writes oh-so-eloquently about gardening in general and vegetables specifically. His series *Produce Farming* on the site is a fount of information.

The URI Cooperative Extension Master Gardeners Web site offers a bounty of information on vegetables: www.uri mga.org.

The New England Vegetable Management Guide is a collaborative effort of members of the extension vegetable programs of URI, University of Massachusetts, and the New England universities. The guide is written for commercial vegetable growers, but I found it helpful.

Their Web site www.nevegetable.org lists crop varieties that are most adapted to New England conditions, along with associated diseases and problems.

If your particular interest is fruit, the Rhode Island Fruit Growers Web site is a goldmine: www.rifruitgrowers.org.

Planting

Some vegetable seeds can be sown directly in the ground as soon as the ground can be worked, such as peas, beets, lettuce, onions, and radishes. Others are seeded directly in the ground only after the danger of frost has passed. If your growing season is shorter, as in the northwestern part of the state, you may need to start plants such tomatoes, brussels sprouts, or cauliflower indoors and set them out when there is no danger of frost.

Seed packets have most of the information you need to know on the back: when to plant, how to care for the plant, and when to harvest it. Each plant has an optimum soil temperature for germination and an optimum soil temperature for growing. A soil thermometer is a handy tool. If the temperature is not right, the seed will either not germinate or the plant will take so long getting established that it becomes weak. And the temperature at which a plant germinates may not be the temperature a plant needs to grow and thrive. The wrong temperature will slow growth or result in a spindly, weak plant susceptible to disease. For instance, tomatoes germinate best at around 60 degrees but grow better at 80 degrees. Lettuce likes cool temperatures; it won't germinate well when the soil temperatures gets above 65 degrees, and it won't germinate above 75 degrees. Pepper and eggplant seeds prefer 85 degrees but the plants grow well at 75 degrees. Harden off your plants before you put them in the ground. See chapter 4 for more seed-starting and cultivation tips.

There are different techniques to planting vegetables: crop rotation, succession planting, interplanting, and companion planting. Each method has sound reasoning behind it. You can choose one approach or combine them.

Crop Rotation

The idea behind crop rotation is that vegetables from the same botanical family should not be grown in the same spot every year. Why? Each vegetable family is susceptible to certain pests and diseases. Insect larvae and diseases often remain in the soil after a crop has been harvested, waiting to attack the same crop the next year. If you plant something from a different family in that soil each year for the next three or so years, you can outwit the enemy. By the time crop number one comes around again, with luck all of that family's enemies will be gone from that patch of soil or at least substantially decreased.

Additionally, different crops use up different nutrients in the soil. If you plant the same crop in the same soil year after year, eventually you will find them getting weaker and weaker because they are deprived of the nutrients they need. You could amend the soil for specific nutrients, but it's easier to rotate. Some crops, like legumes, actually improve the soil; rotating them through the garden will improve the soil in each bed they are planted.

Vegetable families are:

- Alliaceae, the onion family, includes onion, garlic, leek.
- Apiaceae, the carrot family, includes carrot, celery, parsley, parsnip.
- Asteraceae, the lettuce family, includes cardoon, endive, globe artichoke.
- Brassicaceae, the cabbage family, includes broccoli, cauliflower, rutabaga, turnip.

- Chenopdiaceae, the beet family, includes spinach, beets, Swiss chard.
- Cucurbitaceae, the cucumber family, includes zucchini, cucumber, melon.
- Papilionaceae, the pea and bean family, includes hyacinth bean, fava beans, alfalfa.
- Solanaceae, the potato family, includes potato, tomato, eggplant.

Here's a sample crop rotation. Say we rotate through four beds (A, B, C, and D). You plant members of the same vegetable family in plot A the first year, then move the entire family of vegetables (whatever you want to plant from that family) to plot B in the second year, then plot C the third year, and plot D the fourth year, so that they don't arrive back in plot A until year five.

Factor in the height and size of what you're planting so that the crop fits into the rotation but doesn't crowd or block the sun from others nearby. Some vegetables with large foliage (like pumpkins) help suppress weeds. Switching them in rotation will help keep the weed population down. But their large foliage can also create too much shade for smaller plants.

In a crop rotation schedule, you also have to factor in the different pH needs plants have. But plants with different nutritional needs can be planted together—light feeders like carrots work well with heavy feeders like tomatoes.

You will need to keep good notes to remember what you had where from year to year. Planning a rotation schedule, drawing it out ahead of time, and keeping excellent notes will save headaches and frustration in the future.

Succession Planting

Succession planting is simply scheduling one crop to follow another. If you want to have vegetables all season long, you plant an early crop, then a mid-season crop, and then a fall crop so that the garden is in use at all times. It can be of the same vegetable: spring carrots and then summer carrots, which mature in the fall. Or you can plant different vegetables to mature at different times throughout the growing season. The longer your growing season, the more time you have to plant several crops of the same vegetable. An early crop of bush beans, for example, can be harvested and a second crop planted for harvesting later in the season. Don't plant from the same family in the same place more than twice in a season for the reasons given earlier in crop rotation—possible pest and disease contamination of the soil.

The idea is that gardeners don't need to stop planting just because spring has passed. Late-summer planting fills in the holes and takes us through to fall. Just make sure you plant in time for the crop to reach maturity before the first killing frost.

Cool-weather crops are those that do not tolerate heat. They are planted as early-spring crops. Crops such as broccoli, brussels sprouts, garlic, peas, and onions can be planted twenty to forty days before the last frost. Beets, carrots, cauliflower, and lettuce can be planted ten to thirty days before the last frost. Cool-season plants that mature quickly can be sown again in late summer for fall harvest, such as lettuce, peas, and turnips.

Warm-weather crops need warmer temperatures. Sweet potatoes, eggplant, and tomatoes are planted later in the spring, after the soil has warmed to a minimum of 60 to 65 degrees. Snap beans, lima beans, sweet corn, and cucumber should be planted on or after the last frost date.

Interplanting

Interplanting is simply growing two or more crops in the same place. The Native Americans interplanted with corn, pole beans, and squash—the corn became the pole for the beans and a protective windbreak for the low-growing squash. Interplanting makes the most efficient use of space and can cut down on chores which, of course, saves time.

Sow crops that grow at different rates. Plant a slow-growing crop, one that has the potential to take up a lot of space when mature, together with a faster-growing crop that will be mature and harvested by the time the first one reaches maturity. Early beets and winter squash are good examples. Interplanting is also useful when one plant that doesn't like the heat, like lettuce, can be shaded and cooled by the other plant.

Swiss chard, for instance, planted close to tomatoes, shades the soil and helps to moderate the temperature. Deep-rooted parsnips work well when planted with shallow-rooted onions.

Companion Planting

Plants are said to have adversaries and friends that help or harm each other. By clever planting you offer each plant the protection of the other. For instance, the friends to brussels sprouts are beets, bush beans, lettuce, and nasturtium; its adversaries are kohlrabi and strawberry. Friends to carrot are beans, chives, leeks, onions, and tomatoes; its adversaries are celery and parsnip. Louise Riotte has written in detail about companion planting in her two books, *Carrots Love Tomatoes* and *Roses Love Garlic*. Rodale's *Companion Planting* is also an excellent read for more information on the subject.

Tending Your Crops

Tending a vegetable garden is a most satisfying endeavor. And at the end of the day you have delicious, homegrown food.

Watering. Vegetables need regular watering, but the critical times for watering are when the plants are seedlings, when they are about to set flowers, and when they are about to set fruit. Water is essential for leaf and shoot growth, but too much water can slow production of fruit and diminish flavor. Refer to chapter 3 for more details about watering.

Feeding. Test your vegetable garden soil every few years to be sure enough nutrients are available. Certain crops are heavy feeders: Asparagus, cabbage, corn, and eggplant can use an extra boost through the season. Wood ash or bonemeal helps root vegetables. A fertilizer like fish emulsion will incorporate more nitrogen in the soil to benefit leafy crops like lettuce. These fish and seaweed fertilizers are well-balanced natural fertilizers and provide the major nutrients (N-P-K) and a lot of the minor elements, too.

Don't use animal manure on vegetable gardens because of the potential for transmission of disease pathogens.

Weeding. Weeds compete with vegetables for water, nutrients, air, space. Take the time to weed, even if you put in only an hour a day. Don't wait until weeds have gone to seed, or you will be weeding forever.

Keeping plants healthy. Make the garden unappealing to pests and diseases by cleaning up debris and cutting back dead foliage. If your plant is damaged or sick, research what is wrong promptly—before the problem spreads (see chapter 10). Spraying vegetables with chemical fertilizers, insecticides, or herbicides is not a good practice because you are going to put these food plants into your body.

Good soil, sound watering practices, and impeccable hygiene are the best defenses against pests and disease. The end result is a satisfying bowl of homegrown vegetables on the dinner table for your friends and family.

CHAPTER SEVEN

Trees and Shrubs

We plant trees and shrubs for the long term. Thus, selecting the varieties that will adapt happily to your Rhode Island garden is very important. Most trees and shrubs recommended for Zones 5 to 7 will do well someplace in Little Rhody, but research your choices first. That favorite species you've seen growing in Burrillville may—or may not—do equally well at your home on the waterfront at Watch Hill.

What is the difference between a tree and a shrub? For starters, the number of stems, or trunks. Trees have one stem, and shrubs usually have two or more. And size somewhat determines what category a woody plant falls in. The silverbell tree (*Halesia*), for instance, could be treated either like a large shrub or small tree. Some dogwoods (*Cornus* spp.) are multistemmed and look like big shrubs; and franklinia and stewartia are in between. Throughout this chapter I will refer mostly to trees, but you can assume I also mean shrubs unless I state otherwise.

Woody plants, or "woodies," as they are often called, serve many purposes in the landscape.

- For visual aesthetic appeal; to add structure and form.

- For the simple pleasure of relaxing under the spreading branches.

- To create a barrier or hedge for privacy; to keep people out or animals in.

- For utilitarian purposes: to serve as a windbreak, provide shade, or hide an eyesore like an air-conditioning unit.

Soil, drainage, sun exposure, climate, and wind affect the survival of trees and shrubs. Select a tree that is adapted to your site conditions and hardiness zone. "If a plant is matched to the existing environment, it will for the most part require virtually no help to thrive," says James Wilkinson Jr. of SeaScape Lawn, Landscape & Tree Services in Coventry. Consider the cultivar's mature size. Trees and shrubs can get huge! Give a sapling the space it will need at maturity—even if you don't expect to be around then.

Buying a tree is an investment in time and money. It's expensive to remove a mistake. I recommend that you visit an arboretum like Blithewold Mansion, Gardens & Arboretum in Bristol or stroll through the campuses of the University of Rhode Island or Salve Regina University in Newport. This lets you see trees in their mature state, view their foliage in different seasons, or learn about

Rhode Island Rhodies

I never had a fondness for rhododendrons until I visited Gleaner Gardens in North Scituate. Owners Cynthia Gianfrancesco, a URI CE Master Gardener, and her husband, Chuck Horbert, are both environmental scientists. They have opened up their garden to the public because they want to share its breathtaking collection of mature rhododendrons—at least one hundred tagged varieties and many more, different hybrids. "Rhododendrons and azaleas are some of the easiest shrubs to grow in Rhode Island," says Gianfrancesco. Rhododendrons prefer growing in a soil pH of 5 to 6, she notes. Gleaner Gardens is open by appointment; see chapter 12 for details.

tree shapes in winter. Visit nurseries that carry mature stock. Look around the older areas of your town. No matter how gorgeous photos are in books, they don't give an adequate picture of a tree or shrub and its shape in relation to other plants. Do your research.

It's also a good idea to seek the advice of a professional landscape architect, landscape designer, or arborist. You can hire a professional for an hour or two to walk around your property and recommend varieties that suit your property and personality or to visit a nursery with you. You can ask for referrals from you local garden center, request the names of arborists who work at nearby arboretums, or call your town hall to speak to the tree warden in your community. (Chapter 12 lists sources of professional help.)

Great Trees for a Great State

Most tree-loving Rhode Islanders have heard of John Campanini, the founder of the Rhode Island Tree Council. He has studied and worked around trees in this area for more years than he cares to count. Among other things he is a certified arborist, but he simply "loves talking about trees." He maintains a "best of breed" selection, and it was nice to find a lot of my favorites on John's list. You can see many of them growing at Blithewold. Here are just a few of Campanini's best breeds, which are "proven performers and do what they're supposed to do," he states. He adds that these selections handle stress better than their peers. You'll find more recommendations through the council's Web site: www.ritree.org.

Small deciduous trees (15 to 20 feet):

- Japanese stewartia (*Stewartia pseudocamellia*). Beautiful bark. Beautiful foliage. Beautiful flowers.

- Paperbark maple (*Acer griseum*). Shedding cinnamon-red colored bark provides year-round interest.

Small evergreens (15 to 20 feet):

- Hinoki falsecypress (*Chamaecyparis obtusa* 'Gracillus'). Its black green handlike foliage is impeccable. Nice as a shrub but spectacular as a small tree.

- Yellow-thread falsecypress (*C. pisifera* 'Filifera Aurea'). Ropelike yellow green foliage is unusually attractive when this plant is grown as a tree.

Medium-size trees (20 to 35 feet):

- Sargent cherry (*Prunus sargentii*). Cold-hardy tree with beautiful reddish bark and pink flowers.

- 'Heritage' river birch (*Betula nigra* 'Heritage). Vigorous-growing, borer-resistant, white-bark birch.

Large trees (35 to 50 feet):

- 'Homestead' elm (*Ulmus* x 'Homestead'). Oval to round-shaped, disease-resistant hybrid elm that's as tough as nails.

- Katsura tree (*Cercidiphyllus japonicum*). Arching branches and heart-shaped leaves make a beautiful combination.

Extralarge trees (over 65 feet): Campanini calls these "estate-size trees."

- European beech (*Fagus sylvatica*).
- Silver linden (*Tilia tomentosa*).
- Tulip tree (*Liriodendron tulipfera*).

Matthew "Twigs" Largess of Largess Forestry, Inc. (www.largessforestry.com) in Jamestown claims that many Rhode Island native trees are overlooked. "They have been here for 10,000 years, since the last ice age. The New England forest is one of the most beautiful in the world; why not plant it in your yard? Natives are in the *in* crowd." The red maple is the Rhode Island state tree for good reason, Largess asserts: "It adapts to various sites and has great fall color." Largess agrees with Campanini's choices and adds a few of his own:

American beech (*Fagus grandifolia*). This does better in semi-wet to moderately drained locations. It can grow in shade, is smaller than the European beech and longer lived, and is beautiful in winter.

American chestnut (*Castanea dentata*). There are new hybrids of the beloved chestnut trees, famed for their wildlife value.

American hornbeam (*Carpinus caroliniana*). Nicknamed the blue beech, it matures at 12 to 15 feet in height. It likes three hours or less of sun a day, with filtered sunlight. Handsome trunk.

Eastern white pine (*Pinus strobus*). The king of the forest can grow in sun or shade and can reach great heights.

Yellow birch (*Betula alleghaniensis*). Beautiful peeling bark like the paper birch, handsome tree, long life span, can grow in shade, slow growth.

Largess cautions to stay away from the hemlock because of its pest, the wooly adelgid. An infested tree can be treated, he says, "but needs annual treatment, which means high maintenance and cost." Largess believes the hemlock will become extinct in New England. He also discourages planting the nonnative Norway maple, which is "extremely invasive and is banned in some tree nurseries in New England."

The Cary Award

The Cary Award (www.cary award.org) program promotes outstanding plants for New England gardens. Named in honor of Massachusetts plantsman Ed Cary, it highlights home landscape plants that have proven their performance in New England. Visit the Web site to see new and past winners, such as fringe tree (*Chionanthus virginicus*), *Rhododendron* 'Olga Mezitt', and dwarf river birch (*Betula nigra* 'Little King') selected for 2007.

Unusual Evergreens

If evergreen trees are more up your alley, Dave Renzi, a certified arborist and owner of Out In Front Horticulture in Exeter, offers a short list of Zone 6 evergreens. He says these perform well if care is taken to mitigate winter desiccation, or drying.

Cavatine andromeda (*Pieris japonica* 'Cavatine'). Cute as a button and very compact. Adds interest to narrow or tight spaces.

Cherry laurel or "skip" laurel (*Prunus laurocerasus* 'Schipkaensis'). This will fill a niche for interesting evergreen screening or for a columnar effect.

Hollies (*Ilex* x *meservae* 'Dragon Lady' and *I.* x *aquipernyi* 'San Jose'). Two attractive, narrow, and upright-growing hollies.

Leatherleaf viburnum (*Viburnum rhytidophyllum*). Striking in form and foliage, semievergreen, and tolerates more shade than most plants.

Hedges and Screens

A hedge, by definition, is a collection of plants in a row, but "a hedge is a living plant and not a brick wall," says SeaScape's James Wilkinson Jr. Hedges are usually made of shrubs, but you can hedge trees such as beech, hornbeam, and hedge maple.

"Plants have natural form; constantly pruning, clipping, and shearing a woody to the constraints of a straight hedge puts it under a lot of stress," says Wilkinson. As a result they'll need extra TLC. If you want a neat, formal hedge, choose plants that have a tidy habit, and be prepared to groom them twice a year.

Are you trying to enclose a vegetable garden and keep out animals? A thorny shrub may be a good choice. Do you want privacy from the neighbors? You'll want something tall that won't need a lot of fussy pruning.

Do you want evergreen or deciduous? Evergreens stay green and solid, retain a sheared shape better, and look great with a layer of snow, but they grow more slowly. Either you wait years

Favorite Trees and Shrubs for Hedges

I learned a great deal about choosing plants for hedges from SeaScape's James Wilkinson Jr. These are some he recommends for Rhode Island gardeners.

Formal: Beech (*Fagus*), boxwood (*Buxus*), cypress (*Chamaecyparis*), holly (*Ilex*), juniper (*Juniperus*), ninebark (*Physocarpus*), pine (*Pinus*), spruce (*Picea*), and yew (*Taxus*).

Informal: Abelia (*Abelia*), Carolina allspice (*Calycanthus floridus*), cotoneaster (*Cotoneaster*), crab apple (*Malus*), forsythia (*Forsythia*), hawthorn (*Crataegus*), hedge maple (*Acer campestre*), hydrangea (*Hydrangea*), hypericum (*Hypericum*), lilac (*Syringa vulgaris*), mountain laurel (*Kalmia latifolia*), viburnum (*Viburnum*), willow (*Salix*), and witch hazel (*Hamamelis*).

for your hedge to fill in or you start with larger and more expensive plants. Deciduous hedges have a softer form that is gentle in summer, whereas in winter you notice their structure and skeleton, which many people find enormously pleasing. Plants chosen for deciduous hedges grow more quickly and so you may spend less at the beginning. "Deciduous shrubs," says Wilkinson, "recover from damage more quickly. They can also be pruned to the ground if necessary to renew their vigor."

Informal hedges can be planted in a loose row. Choose the more upright of the informal shrubs so that the hedge retains some structure. Rhododendrons look wonderful as a hedge. You can also create a mixed informal hedge composed of different shrubs, but take into consideration the growing conditions of each variety. Lilacs like sweet soil and azaleas prefer acidic; they might have a hard time growing well together.

When pruning a hedge, keep it slightly wider at the base than at the top to ensure that lower branches aren't shaded from the sun by branches above them.

Purchasing and Planting

You can purchase trees and shrubs in four ways:

Bare root: The plant arrives with no soil or very little soil around the roots. It will probably be packed in a plastic bag to keep roots moist.

Balled and burlapped (known in the nursery trade as B&B): The plant was field grown then root pruned and its root-ball dug up with a large amount of soil. The root-ball and soil are wrapped in a fabric like burlap.

Container grown: The plant was started and grown in a pot or container.

Field grown and containerized: The plant was started in the field and then dug up and planted in a container.

The planting rule of thumb for all woodies, whether purchased as B&B or in containers, is to prepare a hole a couple of inches shallower than the root-ball and three times its diameter. Once planted, the tree's root flare—the area where the trunk flares out to the roots—must be above the soil level by about 2 inches. "You must see the flare of the plant above soil or grade level," says Julie Morris, director of horticulture at Blithewold. The single biggest mistake made when planting a tree or shrub "is planting it too deeply and mulching too high," says Rhode Island Tree Council's John Campanini. Oxygen moves downward through the soil to the root hairs. In turn carbon dioxide moves upward into the air. If a tree is planted too deeply, this process cannot take place and the tree may die. SeaScape's James Wilkinson Jr. concurs, noting that when he has been called in to diagnose a failing tree or shrub, one that had been planted in the past five years, "the most common problem we find is that it was planted too deep," says Wilkinson. "Even if the tree or shrub has other issues, often the primary problem is the depth of soil or mulch on top of its roots and trunk."

Plant bare-root shrubs in the late fall to early spring while the plants are dormant. Container-grown or B&B trees and shrubs can be planted any time during the growing season. If you plant in the summer, you'll need to maintain a rigorous watering schedule.

To plant a bare-root tree, keep the roots moist right up to the time of planting. Prepare the planting hole, then create a mound in the center over which you spread the roots.

To plant a balled and burlapped tree, unwrap the root-ball and look for the trunk flare. You may need to do a little detective work and remove soil from the top of the ball to find the flare. Set the B&B plant in the hole and tip it gently to remove the twine and fabric surrounding the roots. If the wrapping is a natural burlap, you can leave the wrap in the hole because it will eventually decompose, but be careful to pull the burlap back or cut it down below soil level.

To plant a container-grown or a containerized, field-grown tree, remove the plant from the container and check the roots. Are they pot bound? If the plant has been in the container too long, its roots may have started to circle around. If left this way in the planting hole, the plant will not survive. You can make several vertical slashes to loosen roots and pry them apart, spreading them around the planting hole. Or you can chop the bottom third of the root-ball off and loosen the roots. Be aware that both these practices stress the tree. The best bet is to stay away from pot-bound plants.

Backfill the hole with the same soil that you removed, not a different soil. Experts recommend that you *not* add any soil amendments except maybe a handful of slow-release organic fertilizer. Plants should come to you in good shape and ready to survive without additional help. Tamp the backfill firmly so that the soil won't settle significantly and cause the tree to sink below grade level. Mulch well, but don't push the mulch right up against the trunk or you will encourage decay. Water the plant into its new home.

Don't prune a tree or shrub at planting time except to remove dead branches. The plant needs its leaf canopy to feed the development of new roots.

Dr. Brian Maynard of the plant sciences department at URI suggests bringing in a professional arborist to install a large tree. "It usually takes two strong people to manage a 4-inch caliper shade tree," he states. (Caliper is measured at 4 feet off the ground.) He thinks it's smart to get assistance even with a 2-inch caliper tree. A 4-inch caliper tree should have at minimum a 36-inch-wide root-ball, he says, which is very heavy. A mishandled tree can be damaged beyond recovery, even though you may not see the effects of damage for years. Professionals have the equipment to safely lift large plants.

Staking

Prevailing wisdom says that newly planted trees should not be staked unless absolutely necessary. Staking has been found to weaken trees over the long term. Left to its own devices, an unstaked tree will establish itself more quickly.

If you must stake a tree, says Maynard, leave the stakes in for as short a time as possible—usually one growing season. Place two stakes at equal distance from the trunk and attach them with something like polypropylene webbing, such as ArborTape, that will not damage the trunk. The webbing should not be so tight that it holds the tree rigid—it is only meant to provide backup until the tree establishes itself. Check twice a year to make sure that the webbing is not strangling the tree.

Watering

Improper irrigation is a common mistake folks make when planting a tree or a shrub. It takes a long time to wet soil, so you should water long and infrequently. (Refer to chapter 3 for a discussion of watering practices.) Water for as much as two to three hours each time, but water slowly—a slow trickle from the hose. Water once a week for new plants and then you can ease off to every two weeks until the plant is well established. It takes time for a new woody to get established, and even a year to two after it's planted you should still be treating it like a newly installed plant. A good rule of thumb is to assume one year of establishment for each inch of trunk caliper. Thus a 2-inch caliper tree should be watered regularly for two growing seasons.

Fertilizing

The best time to fertilize a tree is about one month before root growth begins in the spring, when the soil temperature is above 50 degrees. Depending on where you live in Rhode Island, that would be about mid-March. The worst time is in late fall when the roots aren't growing—it's a waste of time and effort. And the very worst time to fertilize is mid- to late August, when the tree might respond by putting out new growth that could then freeze when the first frost hits.

Tree feeder roots are close to the surface. You can sprinkle organic fertilizer on the soil at the base of the tree working outward, or you can deep-root fertilize with injections of fertilizer toward the canopy drip line. Using a good topdressing of compost or manure will also benefit woodies.

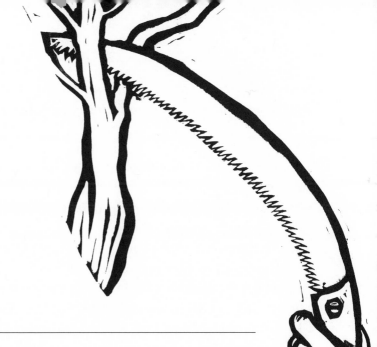

Pruning

I take pruning seriously, because so much damage can be done to a tree if pruned improperly. If you're unsure of your pruning skills, go slowly. Ask yourself if you should bring in a professional. I watched my neighbor massacre a gorgeous old cherry that had bloomed profusely every May. The result was heartbreaking.

There are two reasons for pruning. The first is aesthetic—that is, to improve the look of the tree or shrub. The second is to correct obvious problems: to remove branches that cross and rub against each other or to remove diseased or dead limbs. I pruned my coral bark Japanese maple (*Acer palmatum* 'Sango-kaku') because it had two leaders (main stems). A tree with two leaders forming a crotch may be in danger of splitting at the crotch. I removed one of the leaders so the other could become the main trunk, thereby creating a stronger plant.

Ideally, prune trees in late winter. Insects and diseases are less active then, and as spring arrives the tree will grow and close up the wound. The worst time to prune a tree is in the fall. Trees stop growing in autumn, so wounds will remain open to winter's freezing and thawing, as well as to insects or fungal disease, until the tree resumes growth in spring.

Most flowering shrubs should be pruned in late spring or late winter, depending on the shrub's flowering schedule. Shrubs that bloom in the early spring, like azaleas, are flowering on last season's growth. Pruning them immediately after flowering gives them time to form flower buds for next year's bloom time; prune them in winter and you lose the next year's display. Shrubs that bloom later, say June onward, generally flower on the current season's growth. Some hydrangeas, however, bloom on the second year's growth, so time your pruning accordingly.

Pruning can be done in two ways:

Heading (sometimes called topping) means removing part of a limb, usually closer to the end of the limb. Cut back the limb to a lateral, or side, branch that is at least half the diameter of the limb being cut.

Make your pruning cut flush with the branch collar, *not* flush with the trunk. Cutting too close to the trunk is a common mistake. If the tree limb is large and heavy, make three cuts. The first cut is made furthest from the trunk; cut clean through and remove the limb. Make a second cut a bit closer to the trunk, sawing from the underside of the limb upward, and cutting and only halfway through. Make the third cut flush with the collar for a clean, smooth appearance. This three-step method will prevent the entire limb from breaking off mid-prune and leaving a torn break. It is usually better to remove a whole branch rather than just prune the tips. Study the tree to determine how to achieve your goal (aesthetic or corrective) by removing whole branches back to the trunk.

Warning: The term "topping" can also mean taking the entire top off a tree, so be careful when using that term. This kind of pruning drives arborists crazy, says Largess: "The loss of the crown cuts the tree's food-making ability and it starves. It puts trees in shock from overheating, making the tree highly vulnerable to insects and disease. New limbs that grow back are weakly attached, rapid new growth happens with a far denser crown, and some species die, such as beech trees." He adds that topping makes trees ugly and costly to maintain.

Thinning means taking entire limbs out from the base of the plant or back to the trunk. When thinning to rejuvenate an old shrub, remove only one-third or one-quarter of the plant each year. It may take three to four years to rejuvenate a shrub. This is true for trees also. If you prune too much off at one time, the tree will struggle to survive.

Use the right kind of tools: clean, sharp pruning tools or saws—don't hack at a plant.

Top Plants

Landscape architect Franklin Arts stocks many mature trees and shrubs at his nursery and design company, Earth Scape, in West Greenwich. He has seen all these perform well in the Ocean State:

- **Blue spruce** (*Picea pungens* 'Glauca Procumbens'). This is a creeping, powder blue evergreen.

- **Japanese red pine** (*Pinus densiflora* 'Low Glow'). "Beautiful light green evergreen," Arts says.

- **Plum yew** (*Cephalotaxus harringtonia* 'Fastigiata'). "Narrow, upright evergreen for tight shady spots, and deer resistant."

- **Tree hydrangea** (*Hydrangea paniculata* 'Grandiflora'). This cultivar of the peegee hygrangea offers "clouds of white flowers in summer. Good for a tight area needing a vertical element," he says.

- **Viburnum** (*Viburnum seigneur*). This species attracts birds in the fall with its heavy set of bright orange red berries.

Old wisdom called for dressing pruning wounds, but this is no longer recommended because the plant can't breathe through the dressing, and moisture can collect underneath and encourage disease. The plant is better left to heal itself. Some plants like maples, birches, and yellowwood bleed when pruned in early spring, but this is more unsightly than unhealthy.

There is an art to pruning. I encourage you to stand back and look at the plant. Tie a ribbon around the limbs you are thinking of removing. Step back and imagine the plant without those branches. Will it look better? If pruning is needed for the health of the plant, then you have to make the cuts and live with the consequences. But still try to prune attractively.

Keeping Trees Healthy

There is much you can do to promote healthy tree and shrub growth: Choose disease-resistant species adapted to your conditions. Plant correctly. Practice correct irrigation. Don't overfertilize. Prune in a healthy way.

Sometimes you can do everything right and still have problems, whether caused by drought, wind or sun damage, or insects and diseases. We'll talk more about some of these in chapter 10.

Diagnosing a problem is not easy. You can start by referring to horticultural reference books. You can call in a professional to look at your plant or take a good-size sample (not just one leaf) to your local garden center. You can call the Rhode Island Tree Council (401-861-1995) or the URI Cooperative Extension Master Gardener Hotline (800-448-1011) for advice. Treat your gentle giants with the TLC they deserve.

I enjoy trees year-round. I love their size and beauty, their quiet, enduring quality, strength, and grace. I planted a hedge maple (*Acer campestre*) at Blithewold in memory of my mother, and I am waiting for the perfect tree to plant nearby in memory of my father. Trees evoke deep emotion and a sense of awe.

Lawn

The adage "The right plant in the right place" is every bit as relevant for turf as for any other growing thing. A lawn is not a solid mass of green but a collection of individual plants—about a million plants per 1,000 square feet, writes Stuart Franklin in his book *Building a Healthy Lawn*. The key to a healthy lawn is growing the right grass variety for the climate and then giving it appropriate care.

Lawns look pretty, but they offer more than just good looks. "Lawns cool the air by releasing oxygen, they help control pollution and reduce soil erosion, and they purify and replenish our water supply," explains James Novak of the national nonprofit Turf Resource Center (www.turfgrasssod.org). On a hot summer day, he says, lawns will be 30 degrees cooler than asphalt and 14 degrees cooler than bare soil. "The front lawns of eight houses have the cooling effect of about seventy tons of air-conditioning. That's amazing, considering the average home has an air conditioner with just a three- or four-ton capacity."

Rhode Island Grass

When it comes to turfgrass, Rhode Island is in the know. The Rhode Island turf industry, while not the largest green industry in the state, covers the most production acreage. The University of Rhode Island is a nationally recognized authority on turf, thanks to turfgrass research conducted by the plant sciences department. "The Skogley Memorial Turfgrass Research Facility is the oldest turf research facility in the country," says Dr. Brian Maynard of the plant sciences department. "The turf industry basically owes its existence to research and outreach conducted by URI."

There is a turf to meet every need, depending on your site, your soil, and your requirements for that lawn. Will the grass see high or low traffic—family football games or snoozing? Is it in sun or shade, or a combination? Does your lawn need to cope with salt-laden water and desiccating winds, as in Watch Hill or Block Island, or with the salt lagoons down around Daventry? Do you want perfectly manicured green or a looser, more free-range look?

Turfgrasses are divided into cool- and warm-weather species. Cool-weather grasses grow better in spring and fall and best suit the Rhode Island climate. When temperatures rise in summer, cool-season grasses go dormant and turn brown, returning to green when the heat diminishes. Warm-weather grasses are brown in spring and fall but green up in the dog days of summer.

"Kentucky bluegrass provides the most uniform looking lawn for the New England area," states Glenn Chappell of New England Turf, which is located in South County, the main turf-growing area of the state. But, he adds, "it does need to be cared for to keep it looking nice." Bluegrass is a hardy turf that tends to thrive in the New England climate. It spreads by rhizomes, which enables it to create a smooth, carpetlike appearance. For lawns constantly trampled by active kids, you might add in perennial ryegrass. It's the only major cool-season grass that "combines both superior wear and compaction tolerance," according to the National Turfgrass Evaluation Program. "Mixtures of bluegrass and ryegrass provide sports turf with all the qualities critical for turf that's subject to heavy traffic." In contrast, a yard used only

Cool-Season Grasses

The following cool-season grasses, along with selected cultivars that offer improved aesthetic and disease-resistance qualities, are recommended by URI's College of the Environment and Life Sciences (CELS). For more information download the cooperative extension fact sheets at the Web site of the University's GreenShare Program: www.uri.edu/ce/factsheets/index.htm.

- Kentucky bluegrass. Good Rhode Island cultivars are 'Georgetown' (developed at URI), 'Award', 'Midnight', and 'Blackstone'.

- Perennial ryegrass, especially 'Palmer III', 'Calypso', 'Secretariat', 'Panther', and 'Brightstar'.

- Tall fescue.

- Fine fescues.

- Chewings fescue, including 'Jamestown II' (developed at URI), 'Brittany', and 'Tiffany'.

- Hard fescue, such as 'Reliant II' and 'Defiant'.

- Creeping red fescue: 'Florentine' and 'Shademaster II'.

for weekend barbecues and get-togethers won't necessarily need a high-traffic blend.

Many experts recommend using a blend or mix of grass varieties. The URI fact sheet *Selection of Grasses* states that a "*mix* is made up of two different species of grasses. A typical home lawn seed mix, for example, may be made up of varieties of Kentucky bluegrass, perennial ryegrass, and fine fescues. A mix of these species is generally fairly adaptable to differing site conditions (shade, full sun, dry, moist). Most lawns should be made up of a mixture of grasses appropriate for the particular site. A *blend* is made up of two or more cultivars or varieties of the same species of grass. For instance, a blend of perennial ryegrass might be made up of three or more varieties of perennial ryegrass."

Different grasses have different degrees of adaptability to sun or shade, and dampness or dryness as well as amount of disease or grub resistance. "The best grass for Rhode Island," says John Bannon of the environmentally friendly land-care company Coastal Care in Middletown, "is a blend. A blend is better than a single grass type—a sun mix of bluegrass or a shade mix of anything that will grow in the shade, like a rough bluegrass. It depends on what you want your lawn to do."

Healthy Turf in a Nutshell

- Select the correct grass for your site and requirements.

- Get a soil test done for pH, organic matter, and nutrients.

- Prepare the soil and site. Add soil amendments as indicated by the soil test.

- Seed or lay sod and water in well.

- Do not overwater.

- Fertilize with high-nitrogen fertilizer or topdress with compost.

- Mow at five- to seven-day intervals, keeping the grass 3 to 4 inches high.

- Leave grass clippings on the lawn.

There are countless blends. North Country Organics in Vermont, for example, offers about a dozen blends for different situations, some with clover and some without, some for shade, for grub control, for full sun, for drought. Their Eco-Blend, for instance, contains (in descending order) tall fescue, chewings fescue, perennial ryegrass, hard fescue, Kentucky bluegrass, red fescue, redtop, and white clover. They also offer an Eco-Blend without clover. Clover, far from being a weed, can add nitrogen to the soil. Clover is an excellent additive to grass seed, says Bannon. "It adds texture and remains green long after most grasses turn brown."

But even warm-season grasses may have a place in Rhode Island. They work well for folks who are residents only in the summer months. "If green grass is not so important to you through the spring and fall but you want green grass in the hot, dry summer months only, then you may want to choose warm-season grasses like buffalograss or Bermuda grass," says Paul Sachs of North

Country Organics. Struggling to keep cool-weather grasses green through the summer is a waste of resources.

Turfgrasses are annual or perennial: There is both an annual and a perennial ryegrass, for instance. The annual grasses germinate quickly, the perennial more slowly. And different varieties germinate at different times: Bluegrass germinates in about a month, and tall fescue in three weeks or less. A mix of annual and perennial grasses will give you a combination of grasses that come up quickly and shade the grasses that are germinating more slowly.

Make sure the label indicates exactly what seeds are in the bag. Choose a quality seed. Some cheap mixes may contain a lot of the wrong type of grass for your conditions, or filler, or even weed seed. The lawns of a new housing development near me were clearly seeded with a cheap mix, because sprinkled liberally and evenly over the entire area of good-looking grass is a blanket of the exact same weed—chicory (*Cichorium intybus*)—amusing to me but not to the home owners. And check the packet date: Old seed may not germinate consistently.

Chappell states that a home owner should take as much care when selecting sod as seed. Know what grasses have been used to create the sod you are buying and buy from a reputable turf supplier. At New England Turf they use many types of seed in their blends and mixtures. "We use 100 percent bluegrass, bluegrass/fescue mix, short-cut bluegrass, bentgrass for the golf courses, and many other blends."

Seeding or Sodding a New Lawn

You can use seed or sod to create a new lawn or repair an existing lawn. Either way, the single most important thing to do is to prepare the soil. Rich soil will provide the plant with nutrients to build a strong root system from which leaf blades in turn get their water and nutrients.

Begin with a soil test (see chapter 1) to determine what kind of lawn soil you have, what condition it's in, and if (or how much) the pH needs to be raised or lowered. You'll save yourself some heartache. Turfgrass grows best in a soil with a pH of 6.2 to 6.8.

Incorporate 3 to 4 inches of good loam into the existing soil. You can add amendments at this time if the soil test calls for them—additions such as lime, compost, manure, and a slow-release fertilizer rich in phosphorus (like bonemeal or rock phosphate). Till well and leave the soil loose, free of large stones, and raked smooth. You can fertilize more in the spring, when the grass is well established, with a fertilizer rich in nitrogen, such as cottonseed meal or dried blood.

Seed

How much seed will you need? The rule of thumb is three million seeds per 1,000 square feet. There are about two million seeds in a pound of bluegrass; about 250,000 seeds in a pound of tall fescue. The label on the seed bag should indicate the square footage that bag covers.

Start seeding or laying sod in late August to early September. Temperatures are not too hot and the plants have a chance to get established and strong before cold weather hits.

Broadcast the seed evenly over the area and press the seeds in lightly. Rolling a large garbage can over the area will help with this. Water well and keep it well watered. Keep the area moist, but not soaking wet, until the seeds germinate. Once-a-day watering will suffice unless it rains or the sun is not shining. Continue to water frequently to keep moist, but it is possible to rot the seeds if you give them too much water, so monitor the moisture of the soil. Once the seeds have germinated (which may take up to a month), ease off on the watering but still maintain even moisture. And treat the area gently. Maybe rope it off so that people don't walk on it. Give the area time to get established, and go gently with the first mowing. Remember, these are new young seedlings and lawn mowers are heavy machines.

Starting a new lawn on a slope may require more scrupulous attention to grading, seeding, and watering to ensure seeds get spread evenly and do not get washed away. Watering evenly may be a little tricky, too, so monitor the distribution of water to see how much gets dispersed to the different areas. (See details on watering in chapter 3.)

Sod

Sod usually comes in strips 6 feet long by 18 inches wide. They should be laid with staggered joints, like a brick walkway, so that the strips knit together seamlessly. The best time to place sod is in the late summer and fall. It should be laid within twenty-four hours of being harvested; when ordering sod, make sure the site is prepared and ready to accept the strips. Sod left in a pile will heat up, cook, and die. If you can't lay the sod the day of delivery, water the pile and cover it to keep it moist. Sod that dries out typically will not come back, whereas seed will go dormant and recover when watered or the rains return.

Once laid, water the sod immediately, and water daily for the first three weeks, then frequently after that. Within a month the lawn should be well on its way to being rooted in. Don't water if it rains and don't overwater.

Depending on the growing conditions, you can mow the sod for the first time ten to fourteen days after laying it. But let the soil dry out a little bit before the first mowing so that the mower doesn't push down on the grass. This applies to a seeded lawn also.

The biggest mistake folks make is improper installation of the sod, says Glenn Chappell of New England Turf: Either the site wasn't ready, the sod was not installed in a timely manner, not enough water was used to irrigate, or the sod was put down the wrong way. "Remember," he laughs, "green side up!"

Maintaining a Lawn

A lawn needs water, nutrients, air, sunlight, and regular cutting to keep it healthy—and a healthy lawn experiences fewer disease and pest problems. John Bannon of Coastal Care maintains that the worst thing you can do for a lawn is nothing. "Neglect will kill it for sure!" On the other hand, too much TLC can do the same. It's all about balance.

Watering: In general, apply 1 inch of water a week. Turfgrass in full sun may need more water than turf in the shade, so monitor how deeply the water penetrates the soil (see chapter 3). Regular, deep watering helps establish a deep, drought-resistant root system.

Mowing: Many lawn-care professionals are passionate about mowing. Joe Gibson, a landscape designer and certified horticulturist, owns TrimLawn Lawn & Landscape Services in East Providence. He says the one thing people repeatedly do wrong is mow very short, which opens up the lawn to crabgrass germination. He recommends mowing high. "Three inches or higher, for shade and photosynthesis. Less light is able to reach the soil surface, which means the soil will be shaded and therefore provide less opportunity for weed germination." Higher mowing also provides more grass blade leaf surface; in turn sunlight is more readily absorbed, helping with photosynthesis.

During the growing season a high cut will protect your grass from drought and stress. A higher cut also improves appearance, says Gibson. "It looks thicker from a distance, blemishes are less noticeable, and the grass has a deeper root system." But don't wait until the lawn is *too* long, or the grass blades will fall over, making it harder to get a good cut. You can lower the mowing height when growth slows down as the grass approaches dormancy.

Experts recommend only taking off one-third of the leaf blade at one mowing. Keep your mower blades sharp. Dull blades tear the leaf blade, and that creates a larger surface area which serves as a port of entry for disease.

"Grass clippings are 80 percent water and organic," says Gibson. "They decompose quickly and recycle nutrients back into the soil." Most experts agree that it's good to leave grass clippings on the lawn unless the clippings are too long, in which case they will choke the lawn and look messy.

Fertilizing: Grass plants grow in the spring, using the nutrients stored in the roots from the previous fall. In Rhode Island it makes sense to fertilize in early fall, when the grass comes out of summer dormancy. Fertilize again in mid-fall, when growth slows down, so the turfgrass can store nutrients again for the following year. Some folks like to fertilize around Memorial Day, and while this certainly won't harm your lawn, it isn't the optimum time.

Know your soil and its needs. A light topdressing with a high-quality compost, manure, or slow-release fertilizer is an excellent way to boost the soil. In general, though, what lawns need most are lime and nitrogen. Lime raises the pH level of the soil to make it less acidic. Grass grows best at a pH of 6.2 to 6.8. But don't throw lime on your lawn unless you need it! Your soil test will indicate your lawn's pH and how much (if any) lime is necessary. The normal recommendation is fifty to one hundred pounds of lime per 1,000 square feet applied every two years. The most common source of lime is dolomitic lime.

Wait a week after applying lime before fertilizing. Fertilize just before a good rain or water in the fertilizer so that it doesn't sit on top of the lawn.

Bonemeal can be a useful fertilizer. It raises the soil pH as it helps the grass develop strong root systems the first season. But I am not sure if I would recommend this to home owners with dogs, because, if my dog is any example, they love the smell of bonemeal and roll in it!

Finally, "don't fertilize when the lawn has a disease because it will aggravate the disease," cautions John Bannon of Coastal Care. "Some diseases like fertilizer!"

Green and Healthy

Pests, weeds, and diseases are indications of poor soil and a weak lawn. But don't whip yourself into a frenzy (like I did!) if you notice ugly rings in the grass or see birds pecking at the grubs in your lawn—identify the problem and get advice on how to deal with it.

Lawn Pests

URI offers excellent information on pests and diseases (see chapter 12). Sod webworms, chinch bugs, moles, and grubs are frequently pests in Rhode Island lawns. Of these, the most common pests are grubs—specifically Japanese beetle (*Popillia japonica*), Oriental beetle (*Anomala orientalis*), European chafer (*Rhizotrogus majalis*), and Asiatic garden beetle (*Maladera castanea*). "Lawns that are attacked by these pests show poor vigor, thin turf, smaller to no roots, and bare spots susceptible to weed colonization," writes Stuart Franklin in *Building a Healthy Lawn*.

Many home owners and landscapers battle white grubs without much success because they assume that all white grubs are the Japanese beetle. "They are not!" states entomologist Dr. Marion Gold, director of the URI Cooperative Extension. "Properly identify your grub, and you can select the right method to control them." Some controls include:

Nematodes are microscopic worms that attack insects. Commercially available nematodes are specific to pests stated on the label. The nematode *Heterorhabditis bacteriophora* is an effective biocontrol against Japanese beetle grubs; the nematode *Steinernema carpocapsae* is not. Certain nematodes will work on sod webworms and chinch bugs. Read and follow all label instructions and be certain that the beneficial nematode matches the biology of the pest in question.

Milky disease (*Bacillus popillae*) contains natural bacteria that infect and kill certain species of grubs. Sold commercially as Milky Spore, the bacteria are applied to the soil, where they remain for many years to infect future generations of grubs.

Another "lawn pest" is the family dog. Dog urine is high in nitrogen and can burn turf. Rake out the dead grass and overseed those spots in the fall to repair the damage.

Weeds

Healthy grass is vigorous and will crowd out weeds. Weeds like poor soils, so thwart their efforts by improving your soil. Bare spots in a lawn are an invitation to weeds.

Dealing with weeds can be as painful or painless as you choose to make it. Tim McGuinness at the Olde Bristol Ferry House bed-and-breakfast in Portsmouth finds digging dandelions out by hand relaxing and therapeutic. He deals with weeds before they take over, and his lawn reflects the care he puts into it.

Identify the weeds you have in your lawn, and don't let them go to seed. Weeds can be annual or perennial, grassy or broadleaved. Perennial weeds are hardest to eliminate. At the very least, mow weeds down before they flower. You'll find a list of problem weeds and the correct treatment in chapter 10.

Corn gluten meal has received a lot of press as a weed suppressant. It stops root formation as the plant germinates. It is also rich in nitrogen, which improves the soil.

Commercial "weed-killer" products made from horticultural oils and fatty acids are on the market, but strengthening the soil and therefore the plants is a better way of dealing with weeds.

Accepted practice is to overseed to repair areas that are bare or damaged and to thicken the lawn in the spring and fall; this seems to keep the weeds from starting in the gaps, particularly in sun-shade lawns. Healthy grass will crowd out weeds. Paul Tukey, author of *The Organic Lawn Care Manual*, recommends overseeding cool-season grasses at the same time of year as you would when seeding a new lawn—in the fall. "The new grass will have a chance to settle in prior to winter and will be established enough to tolerate the heat of summer by the following year." Tukey also encourages folks to accept a few weeds as a part of a more natural environment.

Thatch

Thatch is not caused by leaving lawn clippings on the lawn. It is caused primarily by poor lawn care—heavy nitrogen fertilizer applications, watering frequently but lightly, and mowing too short. The result is a build-up of dead and dying grass stems and roots that settle on the soil surface and do not decompose properly. Soil becomes compacted, water does not drain through, and roots reach up to get the water. You end up with an impenetrable mat. A thick layer of thatch creates an environment for disease and pests and can also hamper mowing at the correct height.

Thatch takes years to accumulate. To remove it, aerate the lawn with a core aerator, a piece of machinery that pulls up 2- to 3-inch-deep plugs of soil from the lawn. You can leave the plugs on top of the lawn, like clippings, and they will break down. Aeration opens up the lawn, aiding in water and fertilizer penetration and earthworm activity and thus starting the thatch-decomposition process. You can speed the process by using a thatching rake when the mat becomes workable. The best times to aerate are spring and fall, when grass is growing and not dormant.

Diseases

The best ways to prevent disease are to build a strong lawn and water correctly, in the morning if possible. Choosing disease-resistant varieties of grass will also go a long way to preventing diseases from taking hold. But if you do have a diseased lawn, you should first identify the problem correctly.

Lawn diseases often show up as circular spots in the lawn, and these diseases look the same to the untrained eye. Have a professional diagnose your problem and recommend treatment. These diseases are listed on theURI College of the Environment and Life SciencesWeb site (www.uri.edu/cels) and the at the site of the university's GreenShare program (www.uri.edu/ce/ceec/greenshare .html). While you're online, visit the URI Turfgrass Program Web site at www.uriturf.org.

Common turf diseases include:

- Summer patch: A smoke-colored ring caused by a fungus
- Fusarium blight: Light brown dead spots on the leaf blades
- Leaf spot: White cottony strands near the edge of the dead spot

- Snow mold: Irregularly shaped patches of tan or rusty brown
- Dollar spot: Light brown dead spots on the leaf blades
- Powdery mildew: White powdery covering on the leaf blades
- Red thread: Rust-colored dead patches

Whether you tend your lawn yourself or have a lawn care service help, it's smart to be knowledgeable about lawn care and how you want yours cared for. If you hire a lawn-care company, "hold their feet to the fire," advises John Bannon of Coastal Care. "Make sure they are doing what they say they are doing. Do your research. Check what they're putting on your lawn and how they cut the grass." Beyond that, the watering is up to you and nature.

Invasive Plants

When I started gardening, the last thing on my mind was the problem of invasive plants. As a new gardener I happily planted Japanese honeysuckle (*Lonicera japonica*) and the gorgeous porcelain berry vine (*Ampelopsis brevipedunculata*). Then I learned that these plants were a problem. Lucky for me both plants failed to take hold, and so I felt like I'd been given a second chance. I've since become passionate about the topic of invasive plants.

What is an invasive plant? The Rhode Island Invasive Species Council defines *invasive* as "an alien species whose introduction does or is likely to cause economic or environmental harm, or harm to human health." The council was formed to protect native biodiversity in the state and is an outreach program of the Rhode Island Natural History Survey, the Rhode Island Agricultural Experiment Station, and the University of Rhode Island Cooperative Extension.

To earn the label "invasive," a plant "must be able to compete aggressively and to the exclusion of native species," writes natural resources specialist Thomas Kyker-Snowman in *Downstream*, the newsletter of the Massachusetts Department of Conservation and Recreation Division of Watershed Management. "The worst of the invaders are displacing entire associations of native species and replacing them with alien monocultures." An alarming number of species do extremely well in the wild because they often have arrived in the United States without bringing along the pests that eat them, he writes.

Invasives are opportunists. They can handle tough growing conditions and spread rapidly. Their seeds can be dispersed by birds, wind, or water; on the fur of animals; in the tread of car tires; on your clothes. The statistics about the problem of invasive plants are staggering: Invasives infest more than 100 million acres of land in the United States. Our natural habitats on public land are being lost at the rate of 4,600 acres a day to invasive species. Purple loosestrife now grows in forty-eight states and costs $45 million per year in control and forage loss. State agencies spend millions of dollars on the control of nonindigenous aquatic plants.

"Many ecologists now feel that invasive species represent the greatest current and future threat to native plant and animal species worldwide—greater even than human population growth, land development, and pollution," writes William Cullina, author and nursery manager of the New England Wild Flower Society.

When invasives bully their way into an environment, they change the ecosystem—and biodiversity is lost. Soils change as plants like autumn olive contribute to an overabundance of nitrogen in the soil. This throws soil makeup out of balance. Too much nitrogen will cause plants to grow primarily foliage and no blooms. Aquatic invasive plants choke the waterways and change the chemistry of Ocean State water. Animal habitats are altered if not lost to certain animals entirely. When the native plants are choked out, birds and insects lose food sources. Take the monarch butterfly as one example. "When it lays its eggs on the invasive black swallowwort (*Cynanchum nigrum*) rather than on the closely kin native milkweed (*Asclepias*), the larvae die when they hatch and try to feed on swallowwort," states scientist Lisa Lofland Gould, founder of the Rhode Island Wild Plant Society (www.riwps.org).

An area can eventually become inhospitable to anything that does not support that particular invasive plant.

A plant may be invasive in one area of the country and not in another. Butterfly bush (*Buddleia davidii*), for instance, is invasive in the South but not in New England. But other invasives—such as purple loosestrife (*Lythrum salicaria*)—have spread across the continent. And not every plant that we gardeners call "aggressive" or "a thug" is technically an invasive species in the wild. Thuggish behavior, however, should send up a warning.

Rhode Island's Invaders

The Rhode Island Invasive Species Council has prepared its *Official List of Invasive Plants in Rhode Island*. You will find information at the Web site for the Rhode Island Wild Plant Society (www.riwps.org), the URI Cooperative Extension Master Gardener Web site (www.urimga.org), or the Rhode Island Natural History Survey (www.rinhs.org).

Some states prohibit the sale of certain invasive plants, but no such law exists in Rhode Island. For example, official lists of prohibited plants exist in the neighboring states of Massachusetts and Connecticut. Nearly 150 species are identified as invasive in Massachusetts (see the list at www.mass.gov/agr/farmproducts/proposed_prohibited_plant_list_v12-12-05.htm). The New England Wild Flower Society, in conjunction with the Massachusetts Invasive Plant Advisory Group, published a list of sixty-six critical offenders. Today is it illegal to import or sell nearly all of the sixty-six plants in Massachusetts. (Some exceptions exist for certain ornamental species, which have final sale dates of January 2009.) Connecticut has similar legislation.

"The list of invasive plants in Rhode Island is long," says Carl Sawyer, research associate in the URI plant sciences department. Let's look at some of the Ocean State's primary villains, as identified by the Rhode Island Invasive Species Council. Note that when you see an asterisk, it means that more information is needed on that plant's spread in our state.

Widespread and invasive

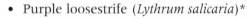

- Fanwort (*Cabomba caroliniana*)
- Asiatic bittersweet (*Celastrus orbiculatus*)
- Autumn olive (*Elaeagnus umbellata*)
- Japanese honeysuckle (*Lonicera japonica*)
- Purple loosestrife (*Lythrum salicaria*)*
- Japanese knotweed (*Polygonum cuspidatum*)
- Curly pondweed (*Potamogeton crispus*)
- Common buckthorn (*Rhamnus cathartica*)
- Multiflora rose (*Rosa multiflora*)
- Black swallowwort (*Vincetoxicum nigrum*)

Restricted and invasive

The term "restricted" means there are prohibitions against planting these plants.

- Tree of heaven (*Ailanthus altissima*)
- Garlic mustard (*Alliaria petiolata*)
- Porcelain berry (*Ampelopsis brevipedunculata*)
- Variable-leaf water milfoil (*Myriophyllum heterophyllum*)
- Lesser celandine (*Ranunculus ficaria*)
- Watercress rorippa (*Nasturtium aquaticum*)

- Wineberry (*Rubus phoenicolasius*)*
- White swallowwort (*Vincetoxicum rossicum*)*

Some aquatic invasives include common reed (*Phragmites australis*), Eurasian water milfoil (*Myriophyllum spicatum*), and purple loosestrife (*Lythrum salicaria*). "Two species that are knocking on Rhode Island's doorstep, and should be watched closely, are Japanese stiltgrass and mile-a-minute vine," adds Sawyer.

Your Choice Matters

If invasives are such a widespread problem, what can we, as gardeners, do? First, look close to home. Do you grow any plants that are on the invasive species list? Many of us planted ornamental invasives years ago, not knowing better. I was sad to see that one of my garden plants, the yellow iris (*Iris pseudocarus*) is on the list. And this is just one garden—multiply that by all the gardens in my neighborhood and extrapolate further. Think of what these invasive plants are doing to every garden, botanical garden, wetland, and natural area. You start to comprehend the enormity of the problem.

Rosanne Sherry, the URI CE Master Gardener coordinator, notes that "if gardeners are more aware of the native alternatives and carefully choose plants in the first place, invasives will be less of a problem." She adds, however, that birds and other migratory wildlife bring some of the invasives, so it will be a never-ending battle.

It was hard to give up my porcelain berry vine, but I saw it as an opportunity to experiment with something new. I replaced the porcelain berry with a golden hop vine (*Humulus lupulus* 'Aureus'), which is great fun.

Eradicate the Invaders

Once invasives are entrenched, it takes a multistep approach to remove them. The trick is ensuring that the invasive plants are removed early, especially young Japanese barberry, multiflora rose, and Japanese knotweed volunteers. Here are steps you can take.

Hand pulling. URI CE Master Gardener Jules Cohen's method of "brute force" seems to be the most common method. I spent countless hours yanking bittersweet out of my trees when we first moved to our home. Lofland Gould in Usquepaugh battles black swallowwort: "It grows rapidly and produces hundreds of windblown seeds; once well established it is extremely difficult to root out." She tries pulling up the seedlings as rapidly as they appear so they won't flower and set fruit.

Establishing barriers, like berms of topsoil covered with heavy-duty landscape fabric.

Not leaving areas cultivated but unplanted. Steve Cotta, owner of Portsmouth Nursery, says that "invasives love nothing more than freshly tilled open plots, and they will almost always be the first to establish themselves if these areas are left unchecked" or unplanted.

Repeated mowing. For plants like Japanese knotweed, Carl Sawyer at URI recommends persistent mowing several times a year for several years. Mow before leaves are fully expanded. This will make a significant dent in a stand. "Persistence is the key!" he says.

Biological controls. Certain insects are known to feed on problem plants. Research is currently being conducted on two species of leaf beetle (*Galerucella calmariensis* and *G. pusilla*) that have been found to feed on the invasive purple loosestrife. Tim Simmons, restoration ecologist with the Massachusetts Heritage and Endangered Species program (www.nhesp.org), said they have "embraced this beetle" wholeheartedly. He visited one site recently where the loosestrife was not just reduced, it was gone! Learn more about the success of this biological control online at the University of Connecticut (www.ladybug.uconn.edu) or Cornell University (www.gardening.cornell.edu).

Chemical controls. Use the big herbicide guns only as a last resort. Many experts who would never normally advocate using chemicals do, in fact, say that sometimes the invasive is worse than the chemical. Lofland Gould in Usquepaugh on occasion gave older black swallowwort plants a direct spray of Round-up because they were too difficult to hand pull. But not all chemical herbicides work on all plants, and different herbicides work on different plants. It is essential that you know exactly what plant you are trying to eradicate and what chemical will work on it. And there is a correct and incorrect time of year to apply herbicides to specific plants.

Be aware: Using herbicides on wetlands is highly regulated by the state—you can't spritz that purple loosestrife growing alongside the stream on your property without a state permit (see

Stop the Invaders!

"My primary advice regarding invasives," says environmental scientist Lisa Lofland Gould, "is *do not* allow them to enter your yard in the first place! Beware of any gardener who says, 'You'll love this plant—it's a real fast grower!'"

- Do not plant nonnative species that are known to be invasive.

- Encourage nurseries to stop selling these plants.

- Do not dig up native plants from the wild to transplant to your own garden—this leaves holes in the natural space, and invasives are opportunists that will fill in those holes.

- Plant more native species—there are plenty of beautiful ones.

- Encourage legislators to create more stringent bans on the importation of nonnative invasives.

- Educate yourself and those you know about the dangers of invasive plants. Spread the word!

www.dem.ri.gov). The herbicide Rodeo, a version of Round-up manufactured for controlled use in wetlands, will kill or cripple every photosynthesizing thing it touches. It must be applied by an experienced person with a state license to use herbicides. You can contact the Rhode Island Nursery & Landscape Association (www.rinla.org) or your local conservation commission to find someone certified to apply herbicides within wetlands.

Proper disposal. Do not put invasive plants on the compost heap. Plants like knotweed can root easily from cuttings, and most compost piles are not hot enough to kill seeds. Some folks put plant debris in a plastic bag and leave it to cook in the sun. The downside of this is that it can take a couple of months for the debris to decompose, and you're never entirely sure if the weeds and seeds have totally cooked. I simply recommend taking the debris to the dump. If you want to burn your debris, check with your local fire department to see if you need a permit. Do not burn poison ivy—the smoke can be toxic.

Elegant Substitutes

The best substitutes for alien invasives are tried-and-true native plants. I think there's a tendency to think that "all native" will mean "all the same" and "boring." Not true! "There are so many beautiful alternatives that people don't even know about," says environmental scientist and Rhode Island Wild Plant Society (RIWPS) member Chuck Horbert. The New England Wild Flower Society, for instance, has more than 1,500 lovely native species at Garden in the Woods, both planted and for sale, and RIWPS offers many at its annual spring plant sale.

Here are some beautiful alternatives to common invasive plants:

Autumn olive: Replace with highbush cranberry (*Viburnum trilobum*) or winterberry (*Ilex verticillata*).

Burning bush: Replace with bayberry (*Myrica pensylvanica*) or red chokeberry (*Aronia arbutifolia*).

Purple loosestrife: Replace with swamp milkweed (*Asclepias incarnata*) or blue giant hyssop (*Agastache foeniculum*).

Of the many other native plants that can be used as replacements, laurel (*Kalmia*), winterberry, fothergilla, dogwood (*Cornus*), sweetshrub (*Calycanthus*), viburnum, and hydrangea are just a few. Visit the New England Wild Flower Society's Web site (www.newfs.org) for a full list titled "Native Alternatives for Invasive Ornamental Plant Species." This list also appears in William Cullina's book *Native Trees, Shrubs, and Vines*, a wonderful read on natives.

"When you need woody landscape plants," says Lofland Gould, "seek out the natives—they are adapted to our soils and climate, and the native wildlife depends on them. And they are beautiful!"

I am still a little surprised by the number of professionals who are unaware of the problems caused by using invasives in the landscape. This is an issue that needs to be addressed, but with compassion—both for the gardener and the garden. Although a very small percentage of nonnative species have become invasive, it would be unwise to avoid nonnatives altogether, says nurseryman Steve Cotta. "To deny the gardener the vast horticultural opportunities represented by the 99 percent of nonnatives that pose no threat of invasiveness in favor of a purely native landscape would be closing the door on a whole world of gardening knowledge and experience that is the cumulative effort of every plant lover since the first gardener walked the earth." You decide for yourself.

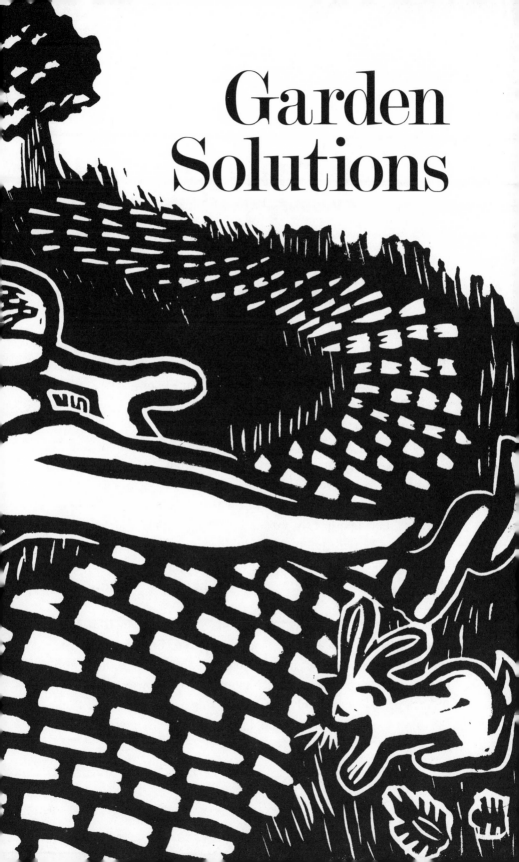

Garden
Solutions

CHAPTER TEN

Coping with Pests and Diseases

If you eat well and get the right nutrition, drink plenty of water, breathe heartily, and live somewhere you are happy, chances are you will be strong, healthy, cheerful, and able to endure tough times. It's the same with plants. They need the right nutrients, water, air, and environment to thrive.

Just like us, plants don't have problems in isolation. Three factors herald the presence of a plant disease. First, a susceptible plant: Plants under stress are more vulnerable to attack. Second, there must be a pathogen: a disease-causing fungus, bacterium, or virus. Third, environmental conditions must favor development of the pathogen. This three-part process is known as the *disease triangle*. The theory is that if you remove just one of the three factors, disease cannot develop.

That's where integrated pest management—IPM—comes in. You may be familiar with this concept. It's a technique for solving the problems of disease and pest damage in a more holistic and ecologically friendly way, with an emphasis on using the least toxic approach. Let's look first at IPM in general terms and then talk about specific garden pest problems and what you can do about them.

Integrated Pest Management

Integrated Pest Management is "a suite of pest-control strategies that allow a gardener to choose the least toxic methods of control," says URI CE Master Gardener coordinator Rosanne Sherry. IPM helps us look to pesticides only as a *last* resort, and not the first choice, she explains. "Many IPM strategies, if used in a timely manner, will in fact easily control the problem." The idea is to find natural ways to reduce pests and decrease the use of chemicals.

IPM does not just involve the control of insects. In actuality, weeds and diseases fit the IPM definition of pest.

When you practice IPM, you tailor your strategy to each pest. There is no one-size-fits-all solution. In each case your choices are based on approaches suited for the plants you're growing (fruit, vegetables, shrubs, flowers), the pest, and your location, according to the USDA Natural Resources Conservation Service. There are many variations on the IPM approach, but they all share these key steps:

1. **Identify the problem correctly.** The first thing is know to what the healthy plant looks like. I once saw an agave that I thought was diseased because it was covered in brown spots. Then I saw the plant name, *Agave virginica* 'Spot', and realized the spots were normal. Knowing a plant's normal, healthy appearance and growth habit will help you recognize when something is wrong.

   Be a plant sleuth. Create a case history for the sick plant. What symptoms does it display—wilted or yellowed leaves? Holes in the leaves? Is the problem on one part of the plant, on new or old leaves, or everywhere? Was the plant healthy when you first obtained it? What are the conditions the plant is growing in? What is the soil like? What is the sun exposure? How much water does it get? Are there sick plants nearby?

Consider these plant problems and their typical symptoms:

- Fungal diseases: Rot, decay, and mold are indications of fungal disease. The entire plant may be shriveled, discolored, and misshapen. Mold can look like a dusting of gray, black, or white flour. There's often a look of soft wateriness to the plants.

- Bacterial diseases: The plant may smell bad, the leaves may be yellowed, curled, stunted, and spotty. Fruits and roots may have soft slimy areas, flowers may be dried up, and stems may be blackened or wilted with wartlike growths.

- Viral diseases: The entire plant may be stunted in growth and misshapen, with yellowing leaves that are mottled and curling with no visible veins.

- Insect pests: Leaves, fruit, stems, and roots may exhibit chew marks or holes. Leaves may drop off. Tiny eggs may be attached to the upper or lower sides of leaves. Flowers, fruits, and roots may be malformed or underdeveloped.

- Environmental factors (drought, road salt, overwatering): The edges of the leaves may turn brown and they may drop. The leaves may be irregularly bleached or mottled.

Sites for Pest Facts

You'll find helpful fact sheets on specific plant pests, diseases, and related topics from these organizations:

- Apeiron Institute for Environmental Living in Coventry (www.apeiron.org)

- New England part of the Northeastern IPM Center (www.pronewengland.org)

- URI College of the Environment and Life Sciences outreach (www.uri.edu/cels/outreach)

- URI Cooperative Extension (www.uri.edu/ce/factsheets)

- U.S. Department of Agriculture (www.usda.gov)

- Nutrient deficiencies can mimic the damage caused by disease. For example, lack of nitrogen may cause leaves to lose some color and turn yellowish; a potassium deficiency may cause leaves to turn grayish green.

2. **Identify the pest.** This is admittedly the tough part—the time when you turn to books, online fact sheets, or experts. My favorite resources are *Mac's Field Guide*, a laminated sheet showing good and bag bugs for the Northeast; *Garden Insects of North America: The Ultimate Guide to Backyard Bugs; Weeds of the Northeast;* and *The Organic Gardener's Home Reference: A Plant-by-Plant Guide to Growing Fresh, Healthy Food.* Talk to an expert at the neighborhood garden center or call the master gardener hotline (see the "Hotline Help" sidebar). You

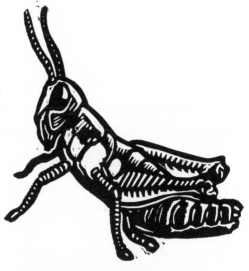

Hotline Help

To get some of your pests and disease questions answered, call the URI Cooperative Extension Gardening and Food Safety Hotline at (800) 448-1011 or (401) 874-2929. It operates March to November, Monday through Thursday 9:00 a.m. to 2:00 p.m.

might want to get a copy of *Insect and Mite Pests of Shade Trees and Woody Ornamentals* written by entomologists Robert Childs and Jennifer Konieczny for University of Massachusetts Extension's Landscape, Nursery and Urban Forestry Program (see chapter 12). Although this was written for professional use, it includes more than a dozen handy checklists that detail when pests are active, and it lists insects and mites by host plant and type of injury.

Remember: Until you know the exact cause of the problem, you won't be able to select the right treatment for the pest.

3. **Learn about the life and habits of the pest.** The idea is to apply treatment or change your cultivation approach at the right time. (Remember the disease triangle.) Insects, for example, are most damaging at certain stages of their lives. The larval stage of Japanese beetles, the grub, devours turfgrass roots; the mature beetle eats certain flowers and leaves. Know when an insect is active so you can apply treatment when the pest is active, not dormant.

4. **Examine the environment.** Does the plant like where it is growing? Have you given it the conditions it needs, including the correct soil, correct sun exposure, proper moisture, enough growing space, good air circulation? Is the area around the sick plant clean, or is there debris that could harbor pests? Break the disease triangle by giving plants good soil and planting them in the right conditions.

5. **Decide how much damage is too much.** How much pest damage can you live with—and how much can the plant handle? Can you live with cosmetic imperfections? If so, you can tolerate a certain amount of pest damage without risking the health of the plant. You can hand pick the occasional yellowing leaf or plant a mildew-prone plant at the back of the border. But if the plant is a prominent specimen in your garden, you'll want it to look good. If the pest is threatening the life of the plant, and you want to keep the plant, you'll need to move to the next step.

6. **Choose tactics to control the problem.** Start with the most environmentally friendly tactic. You have lots of options to chemicals. Tactics include cultural (better garden sanitation, crop rotation, pest-resistant varieties), physical and mechanical (floating row covers, traps, hand picking insects), and biologi-

cal (predators and natural enemies of pests). We'll talk more about tactics later. The point is, only after these tactics have failed should you consider chemical treatment (pesticides).

7. **Monitor and evaluate the results.** Check your garden frequently. Is your pest-control approach working, or do you need to try another tactic? Address new problems as soon as possible so you can treat them with the least toxic method.

Rhode Island Insect Pests

Of the 1.5 million known animal species on our planet, more than 1 million are insects, and fewer than 1 percent of those insects are pests. Even fewer are major pests. Problem insects in the Ocean State include aphids, Asiatic beetles, dogwood borer, Eastern tent caterpillar, gypsy moth, hemlock woolly adelgid, Japanese beetles, lily leaf beetle, locust leaf miner, mealybugs, white grubs, and winter moth. Other common insect pests are chinch bugs, cutworms, earwigs, grubs, leaf miners, mealybugs, mites, moths (and their larvae), spittlebugs, squash bugs, stink bugs, thrips, weevils, and whiteflies.

Here are IPM-oriented tactics you can apply to insect pests:

- Time your planting: Insects usually appear at about the same time every year, so plant to avoid the heaviest feeding stages.

- Determine when a pest is the most susceptible to a control. Control is often easiest at the egg stage, when you can remove eggs from the underside of leaves.

- Protect plants from attack with physical barriers. These can include floating row covers (just make sure you don't trap overwintering larvae under the covers); collars around young plants to stop cutworms; sticky barriers; metal barriers, such as copper strips to repel slugs; and traps—rolled newspapers on the ground to catch earwigs, homemade slug traps, or pheromone (hormone) bags to entice and trap flying insects.

- Attract beneficial insects—pollinators, predatory insects, and parasitoids—as well as birds and bats. (See "Encourage Beneficials," below.)
- Physically remove insects. Hand pick large beetles and caterpillars. Rub off scale. Shake asparagus beetles into a sheet. Lift spittlebugs out of their foam. Prune small branches with tent caterpillars. Spray insects off with strong spray of water if the plant is sturdy enough to handle it.
- Apply an insecticide, but *only* as a last resort.

Encourage Beneficials

As gardeners we differentiate between insects that cause damage in the garden (the "bad bugs") and those that are good for the garden (the "beneficials") because they are pollinators, predators, or parasitoids. Predators or parasitoids attack other insects, explains Dr. Marion Gold, entomologist and director of the URI Cooperative Extension. "Parasitoids are insects (such as parasitic wasps or flies) that live on or in a host insect. The adult female lays its eggs on or in the host. As the young develop, they feed on the host, eventually killing it." Our beneficial garden insects include aphid midges, assassin bugs, bumblebees, common black ground beetles, dragonflies, lacewing wasps, ladybugs, praying mantis, spiders, and wasps.

Most plant-feeding insects and mites can be eaten by some other insect predator, such as a spider, mite, or daddy longleg.

Bad Beetles

The beetle species in Rhode Island that go through a damaging grub stage are Japanese beetle, Asiatic garden beetle, European chafer, Oriental beetle, May beetle, and annual white grub. The Asiatic beetle is much less problematic than the Japanese beetle, while the May beetle can usually be one of the most destructive beetles in Little Rhody.

John Holscher brings in lady-bugs to help control aphid problems at his organic garden center, the Good Earth in Hope. A ladybug can eat more than 4,000 aphids in its life span, which is about a year.

URI CE Master Gardener coordinator Rosanne Sherry cautions that "using insect predators is not a total solution to reducing plant pests in the home landscape, but predators combined with diseases can be useful biocontrols." Here's how to encourage good bugs.

1. Avoid using pesticides. Predatory insects, mites, and spiders are easily killed and repelled by insecticides and other plant-protecting chemicals.

2. Avoid planting garden plants that attract pests. Instead, plant pest-resistant species or cultivars and try to use more native plants.

3. Plant different species. Diversity provides microhabitats and food for various spiders, beetles, and other invertebrate predators. Rhode Island nurseryman Steve Cotta, owner of Portsmouth Nursery, maintains that "it is wise to use a variety of species to avoid a monoculture situation. Should there be a pest, disease, or climate-related disaster, variety is the best way to avoid a total loss." Beneficial insects need protection from the harsh environment that a diversified landscape provides. Use

species with different bloom times, leaf and stem textures, and heights and orientations in the garden or landscape. Leave some of your garden areas unmanaged. Use mulches and ground covers. These practices provide good hiding places for predators.

4. Add plants that attract parasitoids and predators. Plants in the pea family (Leguminosae), aster family (Compositae), mustard family (Brassicaceae), and carrot family (Umbelliferae) offer pollen and nectar for beneficial bugs.

Diseases

Plant diseases are caused by bacteria, viruses, or fungi. These pathogens are transmitted by various means: insects, the wind, rain splashing fungal spores from the ground up onto the plant, and humans. Sad to say, we gardeners inadvertently spread diseases from plant to plant by what is called poor garden sanitation: not cleaning a garden tool after using it on infected plants, touching diseased plants, touching wet plants, discarding diseased plant material improperly, or using dirty pots.

Common diseases in Rhode Island include anthracnose, bacterial wilt, cedar rust, chrysanthemum white rust, daylily rust, gray mold blight, leaf spot, potato wart, powdery mildew, and verticillium wilt. Cotta says that "there are a whole host of fungal infections that can threaten landscape plants in Rhode Island, particularly in the south coastal areas. Phytopthera, rhizictonia, pythium, and botrytis are the most common and can injure roots and foliage as well as completely destroy plants. The best medicine is good drainage, sanitary practices to avoid disease spread, and avoiding plant stress conditions."

URI CE Master Gardener Sybil Parker in Matunuck says she has been victimized by fungal diseases but finds that "a good winter freeze and sanitary conditions seem to keep the fungi from reappearing the next season unless there are extremely favorable conditions."

Certain plant species are host to certain diseases. Hosts for bacterial wilt, for instance, are geraniums and solanaceous crop plants such as potatoes.

To minimize diseases, take steps to break the disease triangle:

- Inspect plants at the nursery to make sure they are healthy and disease free.

- Have regular soil tests done and do whatever it takes to create good soil. A good soil leads to a healthier landscape, and healthy plants are more able to shrug off diseases.

- Choose disease- or pest-resistant plants and buy certified disease-free seed.

- Choose the right plant for your conditions. Give the plant what it needs.

- When planting trees, avoid deep planting because fungal disease in the soil can more easily enter the plant through the submerged trunk.

- Water correctly, optimally at the base of a plant (see chapter 3). Water in the early part of the day so the leaves have time to dry before cooler evening temperatures.

- Avoid touching wet plants, when possible. "Never prune a plant when the foliage is wet," says Steve Cotta. Wash your hands or tools after touching a diseased plant. Clean tools regularly, and *always* after using them on a diseased plant.

- Rotate your crops (see chapter 6).

- Don't overcrowd your garden. Allow for good air circulation to prevent dampness and fungus.

- Keep the garden tidy to eliminate habitat for pests and disease.

- Remove the infected part of a plant or the entire plant. Dispose of diseased plants appropriately—you can bag them and leave them in the sun to cook, but since you can never be entirely sure that the pathogens have been destroyed, I would just as soon take this kind of garden debris to the dump. Do not compost diseased plant material. Adds Cotta: "Many fungal outbreaks can be reduced or eliminated by removing leaf and dead flower debris from around the base of plants."

For organic gardener and designer Kim Lamothe of Green Lion Design based in Tiverton, the solution to pest and disease problems is clear: "To prevent disease, build a healthy garden."

Weeds

Weeds compete for everything in the garden—space, nutrients, moisture, sunlight, air. There are annual weeds, perennial weeds, grassy weeds, broadleaf weeds, woody weeds, and vining weeds. I counted twenty-six "typical Rhode Island weeds" in the URI *Rhode Island Sustainable Gardening Manual.* They include chickweed, crabgrass, carpetweed, purple deadnettle, shepherd's purse, lamb's-quarters, wild carrot, wild garlic, white clover, and oxalis.

Know what weed you are dealing with, because different weeds respond to different controls. A useful book is *Weeds of the Northeast* (see chapter 12). Hand pulling may be fine for a summer annual like pigweed (*Amaranthus*) but may never get rid of perennial Japanese knotweed (*Polygonum cuspidatum*).

Susan Estabrook manages a URI CE Master Gardener project at the historic property Prescott Farm in Middletown. She encourages the volunteers to learn their weeds and if they are edible to pick and eat them. A good reference book on this subject is the Peterson field guide *Edible Wild Plants.*

The URI manual mentioned above offers some methods for eradicating common weeds, and the URI Cooperative Extension Master Gardener Web site provides links to sites that offer detailed information (www.urimga.org).

Here are strategies for common weeds.

Grassy summer annuals: crabgrass, goosegrass, foxtails, and barnyard grass. Hand pull them, trying to remove all of the root. Do not aerate the lawn or garden when crabgrass is germinating, as it will bring weed seeds to the surface.

Broadleaved summer annuals: lamb's-quarters and prostrate spurge. Mow high to shade out germinating and emerging weeds.

Grassy winter annuals: annual bluegrass. Mow flower heads to prevent seed production. Correct compacted soil.

Broadleaved winter annuals: chickweed, shepherd's purse, and purple deadnettle. Hand pull, making sure you get all the roots. Mow to prevent flower heads from forming.

Grassy perennials: yellow nutsedge, quackgrass, horsetail, and tall fescue. Remove clumps, including the entire root system. Aim to control during the first year of growth.

Broadleaved perennials: dandelion, oxalis, white clover, and Canada thistle. Mow high so the turf can outcompete the weeds. Mow the flower heads to prevent seed production.

You can reduce the amount of weeds that get started in your garden by cultivating less vigorously. Deep cultivation brings weed seeds to the surface: *If they need light to germinate, then you've just brought them back to life.* Cultivate in a way that loosens and aerates the soil but does not turn it over too much. One such way is to drive in a fork and wiggle it gently back and forth.

Mulching also reduces weed growth. Additional ways to eliminate weeds include hand digging, burning with a flamer, or planting so closely that weeds are shaded out. As a last resort (and often used just for invasive plants) are herbicides.

Keep weeds down—they compete with your landscape plants for everything. But you've heard the saying "A weed is just a plant in the wrong place." Some "weeds," like long meadow grasses, do provide a home for wildlife, and weeds like clover and daisies provide a food source for beneficial insects.

Big Pests

Deer, rabbits, voles, moles, and other furry creatures are common garden pests. Their damage is usually easy to identify. Moles tunnel to eat grubs in the soil; voles eat plants from the roots up. Rabbits leave a sharp-edged 45-degree cut when they eat nibble off vegetation. You'll see narrow teeth marks where rodents like mice have eaten. Deer feed on new, succulent growth and rub antlers against trees. In winter they eat evergreens and strip bark. Take a quick look at the URI GreenShare animal pest fact sheet and you'll find bats, deer, moles, rabbits, skunks, squirrels, chipmunks, voles, woodchucks, and woodpeckers to be common pests.

Some critter controls include:

- Protect plants from attack with physical barriers. These can include electric fences, sonic devices to deter moles, rabbit fencing, and deer netting 8 feet tall or higher.

- Apply contact repellents or area repellents to make plants less palatable. Think "repel," not "kill."

- Select plants that are unattractive to deer—although as far as I can tell, hungry deer will find anything attractive. Horticulturist Dave Renzi of Out In Front Horticulture in Exeter claims that in his experience deer avoid boxwood. Leucothoe and andromeda (*Pieris*) species are also pretty deer resistant, he adds. "Deer will nibble to test but usually leave them alone."

Arborvitae is a favorite deer snack in winter. URI is testing an arborvitae replacement that seems to be deer resistant: the California incense cedar (*Calocedrus decurrens*). "It's a beautiful conifer that is rare but grows really well in our area," says Dr. Brian Maynard of the university's department of plant sciences.

Grace McEntee, an author and herbalist living on Prudence Island, sees something positive in the actions of pests. She laughs, saying that vole holes improved the drainage on her property!

Pesticides, Insecticides, Herbicides

Under the environmentally friendly IPM approach, apply pesticides or herbicides as the last resort. If you must reach for a toxic spray, try a natural or botanical product first. Use all chemical treatments carefully, even those labeled organic. Although botanical controls are derived from naturally occurring sources, *even they are not always safe for other plants, animals, and beneficial insects.* You could just as easily hurt or kill good bugs in the garden as bad bugs.

Diatomaceous earth is crushed fossilized skeletons of marine creatures. The razor-sharp particles pierce soft-bodied creatures like slugs, beetles, aphids, and spider mites so that insects dehydrate. Diatomaceous earth is effective only when dry.

Horticultural oil is made from petroleum. It suffocates insects.

Insecticidal soap is made from potassium salts of fatty acids. It induces dehydration.

Milky disease (*Bacillus popillae*), sold commercially as Milky Spore, is made of bacteria that attack some but not all grubs. Once applied to the soil, it remains in the soil, continuing to infect grubs for many years.

Bt (*Bacillus thuringiensus*) is used to control caterpillars and beetles. Bt is an insecticidal baterium. It causes the breakdown of cells in the insect's gut.

Beneficial nematodes are microscopic worms that attack certain insects; different nematodes treat different insects.

Neem, a botanical derived from the neem tree, interrupts an insect's hormonal activity.

Pyrethrin compounds derived from chrysanthemums are among the most common ingredients in organic pesticides these days. To be effective these compounds must come into direct contact with the pest within about one hour of application.

Rotenone is a botanical poison made from the root of a tropical plant that can be toxic to fish and aquatic organisms. You need a permit from the state to use it near water or wetlands.

No matter what pesticide you use, natural or synthetic, *always read and follow the label*. Be certain that what you are applying matches the biology of the pest you are trying to control.

IPM at Work

URI research associate Carl Sawyer maintains that pest management has a great deal to do with plant vigor. "Whatever can be done organically to promote healthy plants will have a beneficial effect on pest control."

Joyce Holscher of the Good Earth organic garden center in Hope simply says, "Feed the soil." She adds compost to boost the soil and plant health. Adding to the soil *below* problem plants rather than fertilizing plants usually works and prevents the pests from attacking forced new growth from overfertilization.

Do not fertilize plants that have disease or insect infestations.

An IPM Garden in Glocester

Organic gardeners Kristin Howard and Erbin Crowell, members of the Rhode Island chapter of the Northeast Organic Farming Association (NOFA/RI) set up their gardens in Glocester as 8-by-24-foot strips with grass paths in between. "We have a portable chicken coop (chicken tractor) that we move between the beds," says Howard. "The chickens clean out the weeds, weed seeds, leftover plants from the previous year, and grub larvae, and they fertilize the beds." Howard and Crowell also have a polyculture bed where they interplant vegetables with flowers and herbs to confuse pests. "This bed produced better carrots than our carrot bed this past year," notes Howard.

"Some diseases get stronger with fertilizer," says John Bannon of Coastal Care in Pawtucket. You may think that a quick boost of plant food will help the plant, but all that does is create a flush of tender growth that the pest attacks with gusto.

You should always provide the proper conditions the plant needs, notes URI CE Master Gardener coordinator Rosanne Sherry. Plants grown in sun that prefer shade will ultimately be unthrifty or fail altogether. Be sure the water and fertility needs are met. "Don't plant something because it's pretty. Plant something because it's appropriate for the location. Consider the larger environment or habitat that the plant is growing in." She adds that sustainable plants are wise choices of plants selected for their characteristics. "These characteristics include low inputs of resources like water, few if any chronic pest problems, may be native or at least well behaved and adapted to the climate and soil conditions of the area."

Don't forget to check hardscape structures; these are often overlooked as hosts to pests. You may find tiny eggs on the bottom of shingles that later become mature and destructive insects. If you have an insect problem, then learn what that insect looks like at each stage of its life cycle.

Cultural practices, such as pinching bad leaves and providing good air circulation around susceptible plants, are your best bet for preventing fungal diseases.

Steve Cotta says the best advice he can give any gardener is to educate yourself. "The world of plants can be mysterious, and Latin names may be confusing, but the rewards of knowledge are well worth any effort given. Read books, talk to experts, and learn from your own experiences."

Like these folks you can reduce pest and disease damage by practicing integrated pest management. Keep your own garden free of these "enemies" and plant intelligent, sustainable landscapes. You *will* help the big picture.

C H A P T E R   E L E V E N

Special Challenges: Seaside and City Gardens

Rhode Island has so much coastline that I would not do the state's gardeners justice if I didn't talk about gardening at the seashore. But as an ex–city girl, I am also partial to gardens in town. To round out *The Rhode Island Gardener's Companion*, I address both "flavors" of gardening, each with special needs.

Seaside Gardening

All folks who garden by the sea face similar challenges—salt and wind. And given that there are 400 miles of coastline in Rhode Island, it's no surprise that there are many seaside gardeners in the state. There are islands, salt marshes, rocky shores, wetlands, beaches, cliffs, dunes, salt ponds—you name it and most Rhode Islanders are probably close to it. Doug Hoyt out on Block Island, for instance, gardens at his home high on a hill. It has a great view, but plants get battered by salt wind.

Anne Wilson suffers similarly at the seaside garden she has

maintained for eighteen years in Newport just off Ocean Drive. It is very exposed on a rock ledge, which causes drainage problems. But the biggest challenge for her too is the wind. "Coming from the west it's not too bad, but from north, northeast, or south, it's bad." They have planted living barriers in the form of privet hedges which, she maintains, "are dense enough that they do help block the wind and are hardy enough to cope with the salt brought in on the wind."

Rhode Islanders can learn about seashore gardening at their own thirty-three-acre botanical garden, Blithewold Mansion, Gardens & Arboretum in Bristol, overlooking the Naragansett Bay. It's one of only two arboreta in the country situated on salt water. Visitors can see plants that survive and thrive in those conditions. In particular the rock garden down close to the water gets hit by wind and drenched with salt water every so often; anything growing there is an example of a great seaside plant.

Designing a Seaside Garden

How can seaside gardeners cope with their intrinsic challenges? Heather Driscoll is head gardener at Carnegie Abbey Club, a private sporting estate in Portsmouth, across the bay from Blithewold. In a garden without the wind buffer of a house or even a shed, she says, sturdy plants like hydrangea and shorter varieties of ornamental grasses move to the top of her list. "Add some 'Stella D'Oro' daylilies and hardy pink geraniums, and you have a simple but classic seaside garden." She also chooses perennials with strong root systems to withstand coastal winds. "Rudbekia 'Goldsturm' and bee balm have been proven winners," she says.

Right Plant, Right Site

I recommend the book *Coastal Plants from Cape Cod to Cape Canaveral*, written by two Rhode Islanders, the late Irene H. Stuckey and Lisa Lofland Gould (who also founded the Rhode

Island Wild Plant Society). It describes in detail the different habitats you encounter by the sea. The two authors stress that knowing what kind of place a plant wants to be in—and then putting it there—goes a long way toward ensuring that plant's happiness. And a happy plant needs less maintenance.

Perfect Seaside Plants

June Halliday manages the perennials nursery at Chaves' Gardens & Florist in Middletown. She fields frequent questions from customers looking for plants that withstand seashore conditions. Her own garden in Jamestown has become a personal laboratory for these kinds of plants. As a bonus, most of the following plants are not bothered by the deer that roam around her property.

Shade and part shade

- Bleeding heart (*Dicentra formosa* 'Luxuriant', *D. spectabilis*)
- *Hakonechloa* 'Aureola'
- Japanese painted fern (*Athyrium filix-femina* x *niponicum* 'Branford Beauty')
- Lenten rose *(Helleborus orientalis)*
- *Ligularia* 'The Rocket', 'Brit Marie Crawford'
- Lungwort (*Pulmonaria* 'Benediction')

Woodland

- Bunchberry dogwood (*Cornus canadensis*)
- *Phlox divaricata* 'London Grove Blue'
- *Spigelia marilandica* 'Indian Pink'
- Virginia bluebells (*Mertensia virginica*)

- Wild ginger (*Asarum canadensis)*

Sun (very long blooming)

- Black-eyed Susan (*Rudbeckia* 'Herbstonne')
- Cranesbill (*Geranium* 'Rozanne')
- Pink (*Dianthus* 'Rosish One')
- *Salvia* 'May Night'
- *Veronicastrum* 'Fascination'

Anne Wilson reels off a list of perennials that do well for her at the garden on the ledge: "*Alchemilla* everywhere. Irises, Japanese iris, thalictrum (lots of different ones), cimicifuga, toad lily, hostas of any sort, different hydrangeas like 'Nikko Blue', ajuga. Pachysandra does well in summer but dries out in winter depending on location." Other "old standbys" include *Hakonechloa, Houttuynia* ground cover, ginger, and variegated Solomon's seal.

Heather Driscoll in Portsmouth finds from experience that plants with gray foliage like santolina or artemisia perform well by the sea. Here are seaside plants she likes:

- Bearded iris
- Coreopsis
- Hydrangea
- Montauk daisy (*Nipponanthemum nipponicum*)
- Obedient plant (*Physostegia virginiana*)
- Sea holly (*Eryngium maritimum*)
- Sea lavender (*Limonium latifolium*)
- Sedum
- Thyme

These are some of my favorite seashore plants:

- Black fountain grass (*Pennisetum alopecuroides* 'Moudry')
- *Chrysanthemum* 'Sheffield Pink'

- Daylily (*Hemerocallis* 'Happy Returns')
- Leatherleaf sedge (*Carex bucchanii*)
- Miscanthus (*Miscanthus sinensis* 'Morning Light')
- Panic grass (*Panicum amarum* 'Dewey Blue')
- Pine (*Pinus thumbergii* 'Thunderhead')
- Russian sage (*Perovskia atriplicifolia*)
- Spruce (*Picea pungens glauca* 'Montgomery Blue')
- Stonecrop (*Sedum spurium* 'Dragon's Blood')

Indestructible Seashore Plants

- Beach wormwood (*Artemisia stelleriana*)
- Beach grass (*Ammophila*)
- Seaside goldenrod (*Solidago sempervirens*)
- Bearberry (*Arctostaphylos*)
- Beach plum (*Prunus maritima*)
- Bayberry (*Myrica cerifera*)
- Shadblow (*Amelanchier*)
- Juniper (*Juniperus virginiana*)
- Groundsel tree (*Baccharis halimifolia*)

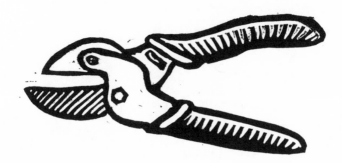

City Gardens

If you're living in town—whether it's Providence, Newport, Bristol, Woonsocket—you will undoubtedly be gardening in a smaller space than folks in suburban and rural sections of the Ocean State. But this can be a blessing. Gardeners with large plots rarely sit and relax in their gardens because there's always so much work to be done. With a small garden, you can do the spring clean-up one day, shop for plants and get them in the ground the next day, and mulch the beds on the third. On day four you can put up your feet, sip a glass of wine, and enjoy the fruits of your labor!

Possibly the most challenging element of urban gardening is the soil. Rich Pederson, farm manager of certified organic City Farm in Providence, says they are always working to improve the soil and protect from pollution. A soil test is essential if you plan to grow food crops. Urban soil is often exhausted, too—devoid of nutrients and laden with castoff debris. (Turn to chapter 1 for a refresher on improving soil.)

Buildings and streets hold in the heat and can deflect or redirect wind so an urban garden may provide a broader array of microclimates, enabling you to grow plants with a warmer zone rating than your friends in the suburbs can grow. Garden designer Susan Champagne in Newport grows heat-loving plants in a strip of garden squeezed between her house and her neighbor's. On the flip side, the extra heat—or the channeled wind between buildings—may cause plants to dry out rapidly.

Designing a City Garden

Just as you would with a larger garden, get to know your site: the pattern of sun and shade through the day and the growing conditions. Determine how you want to use your garden—for entertaining, relaxing, playing, or exercising? What are your privacy concerns? Do you want your garden completely screened from the street, or do you enjoy passers-by peeking at your handiwork?

Because they are compact, urban gardens are sometimes easier to envision. You may be able to design your garden entirely from a second-floor bedroom window, as did Susan Pasquarelli in Newport. "I could see the whole garden in one viewing," she reports.

Think of your small space as a frame within which you paint with plants. Your canvas may be small, but your palette doesn't have to be. You can make bold choices. Look at what you have: an interesting garage wall, lovely old trees next door, an antique fire escape, a rustic fence or hedge, or a great set of front steps that lead directly onto the street. Incorporate these hardscape elements into your design.

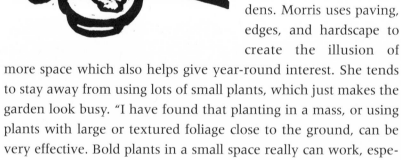

When not at work as director of horticulture at the thirty-three acres of Blithewold Mansion, Gardens & Arboretum in Bristol, Julie Morris works in her tiny garden in town. She asserts that hardscape is almost more important in small gardens. Morris uses paving, edges, and hardscape to create the illusion of more space which also helps give year-round interest. She tends to stay away from using lots of small plants, which just makes the garden look busy. "I have found that planting in a mass, or using plants with large or textured foliage close to the ground, can be very effective. Bold plants in a small space really can work, especially as accents."

Container gardening is ideal for people who may have only a deck or patio. Group the containers creatively to build a garden without having to plant in a bed. Stagger the height of the containers, place them on steps, or hang them from fences, walls,

Containers in the City

Susan Champagne designs many of the containers at the Farmer's Daughter in South Kingstown. Her beautiful city garden in Newport is a showcase for many gorgeous and unusual containers and has been featured in magazines. Here are some of her favorite container plants:

- Alligator weed (*Altenanthera ficoidea* 'Red Threads'). Finely cut dark leaves make a great textured plant for window boxes or containers. Sun to shade.

- *Coleus* spp. Great texture and foliage with large and small leaves. Sun to shade.

- Fiberoptic grass (*Scirpus cernuus*). Great draped over the edge of a pot. Prefers sun.

- Flax lily (*Phormium* 'Apricot Queen'). Wide blades with apricot centers give height and texture in a container. Prefers sun.

- *Impatiens* Fusion series. "Not your Grandmother's impatiens," Champagne says. Wonderful soft colors of peach, yellow, and apricot that have flower power all season. Sun to shade.

- *Melianthus major* 'Honey Flower'. Large, coarse gray leaves are deeply serrated and dramatic. "It will not bloom in our zone, but wonderful height and foliage for containers." Full sun.

- *Plectranthus* 'Lemon Twist'. Soft lime-colored edges, great texture. Sun or shade.

- Scented geranium (*Pelargonium* 'Splendide'). Lovely scent, beautiful tiny grey leaves, and dainty cranberry flowers. Full sun to light shade.

- Spurge (*Euphorbia* 'Diamond Frost'). Sweet white flowers that bloom all season long. Sun to partial shade.

- Wandering jew (*Tradescantia zebrina* 'Purple Heart'). Great purple texture with a tiny purple flower. Sun to shade.

Plants for Small Spaces

Landscape architect Franklin Arts owns Earth Scape in West Greenwich. When he is not designing gardens and installing plants, he is at his nursery tending his plants, many of which he recommends for small spaces.

- **Beech:** *Fagus sylvatica* 'Rohan Obelisk' is a narrow tree with red foliage.

- **Cypress:** *Chamaecyparis nootkatensis* 'Strict Weeping' is a narrow evergreen.

- **Japanese maples:** *Acer palmatum* 'Shindeshojo' has leaves that emerge pink in spring and turn green in summer; *A. palmatum* 'Twombly's Red Sentinel' is a narrow tree with red foliage.

- **Spruces:** *Picea glauca* 'Pendula' is a narrow, blue green evergreen; *P. omorika* 'Pendula Bruns' is narrow and silvery green; and *P. pungens* 'Sester Dwarf' is powder blue.

porches, overhangs, screens, and trellises. In a small space, where the eye is drawn to colorful flowers or foliage, containers allow you to make changes quickly. When one plant stops blooming, you can exchange it for something else. Or you can rely on foliage colors and textures to make a statement.

Great City Plants

Often your plant choices in a city garden are determined by how much light your garden receives. Designer Susan Champagne of the Farmer's Daughter in South Kingstown had to contend with two big old trees in her Newport neighbor's yard that almost completely blocked the sun from her garden. With her neighbor's go-ahead, she pruned the trees but still found little sun getting through. Undaunted, she incorporated unusual shade plants into her design and hung plants on the walls to catch what sun there is. She took a limitation and made of it an elegant garden for evening cocktails and dinner.

Shrubs and small trees will grow in containers, especially if you have space in a garage or basement to overwinter them. You also can keep a larger shrub small by means of judicious pruning.

City gardeners don't have to go without home-grown produce or herbs. Tomatoes, peppers, beans, strawberries all thrive beautifully in pots. Different lettuce varieties make a gorgeous display when grouped together. Don't be afraid to interplant vegetables with nonedible flowering plants, or edible flowers would be even better. Don't forget the herbs like parsley, oregano, chives either—they thrive in pots, too.

Encouraging Wildlife

Wildlife has a place even in a city. Birds and butterflies bring life and whimsy to a garden. Bird-loving URI CE Master Gardener coordinator Rosanne Sherry suggests incorporating a water feature to attract wildlife. Water elements are also very soothing, she says. She recommends some specific ways to attract birds and wildlife to your garden.

- Plant vegetation of different species, growth habits (height, color, plant form), and bloom times.
- Include several nut-bearing or fruit-bearing trees and shrubs to attract birds. Birds particularly like dark berries.
- Allow space for tall herbaceous plants, including grasses and even weeds! These provide nectar for beneficial insects and hiding places for ground-dwelling creatures.
- Plant shrubs and evergreens and include rock walls or rock groups. These give birds and other wildlife protection from predators and harsh winter winds.
- Add a water source, such as a birdbath.

And you can attract birds and other wildlife by putting out birdseed, suet, and other appropriate foods.

A city garden can accomplish a lot in a compact space. A single garden accessory will give a pocket garden drama whereas it may get lost in a huge landscape. Incorporate views into your garden for your neighbors and you improve the aesthetic of your neighborhood. Nothing beats strolling around a city and gazing over garden gates. Take the famous annual Secret Garden Tour in Newport and you'll see what I mean.

As a gardener you are blessed whether you live in the city or by the shore or in the city. The challenges of starved soil and pollution in the city or sandy soil, wind, and salt along the shore are worth surmounting to reach your gardening goal. And I'll be out looking to see how you did it.

CHAPTER TWELVE

Resources for the Rhode Island Gardener

Rhode Island offers a bounty of gardening resources, and this chapter gives you a sampling. But perhaps some of the best resources are your neighborhood garden centers and your local garden clubs. There are a lot of good gardeners in Rhode Island—talk to them! You can also learn from horticultural societies, master gardener associations, garden clubs, workshops, flower shows, lectures, plant sales, and organized garden tours.

University of Rhode Island

The University of Rhode Island (URI) has one of the finest environmental sciences, plant sciences, and horticulture programs in New England, not to mention a fabulous botanical garden and a campuswide self-guided tree walk (see the listings under "Public Gardens"). URI is a terrific resource for gardeners. The College of the Environment and Life Sciences (CELS) is home to the Department of Plant Sciences and Entomology, the Cooperative

Extension (CE) and its Education Center (CEEC), the GreenShare program, the Home*A*Syst water program, sustainable landscaping, the master gardener program, and more. The CEEC is on the campus at 3 East Alumni Avenue, Kingston 02881. There are volumes of fact sheets available about every aspect of gardening. Call the CE Education Center at (401) 874-2900 or visit the specific Web sites to get the information you're searching for:

College of the Environment and Life Sciences (CELS): www.uri .edu/cels

CELS Department of Plant Sciences and Entomology: www.uri .edu/cels/pls

GreenShare program and gardening fact sheets: www.uri.edu/ce/ factsheets/index.htm

Healthy Landscapes program (landscaping for clean water): www.uri.edu/ce/healthylandscapes

Home*A*Syst program: www.healthylandscapes.org or www.uri.edu/ce/wq/has

URI Cooperative Extension: www.uri.edu/ce/ceec

URI Cooperative Extension Master Gardeners: www.urimga.org

URI Sustainable Communities Initiative: www.uri.edu/sustainability

URI Turfgrass Program: www.uriturf.org

And let's not forget Dr. Marion Gold, entomologist and director of the URI's Cooperative Extension Education Center, who is also the Plant Pro on NBC/Channel 10. Her popular and much-viewed gardening segments are broadcast from the URI greenhouses and air regularly.

URI Cooperative Extension Master Gardeners

Master gardeners are educated, trained volunteers who help the public with their gardening problems. To become certified they must attend a forty-hour training course and then contribute an equal number of hours in volunteer time to the community. The URI Cooperative Extension Master Gardeners keep their skills polished through additional training and volunteer work each year. For help with your gardening problems, or to find out more about becoming a URI CE Master Gardener, call the toll-free hotline at (800) 448-1011; it operates 9:00 a.m. to 2:00 p.m. Monday through Thursday, March to November. Or visit the Web site (www.urimga .org). The hotline is staffed by trained Cooperative Extension Master Gardeners.

University of Massachusetts Extension

Many Rhode Island gardeners get a lot of information from the UMass Extension Web site (www.umassextension.org). You'll find specific plant information, all sorts of fact sheets and print materials, and details about events. The extension service is headquartered on the campus of UMass Amherst; (413) 545-4800.

Flower Shows

Newport Flower Show (401-874-1000; www.newportmansions .org). The Preservation Society of Newport County, which owns and runs the Newport Mansions, puts on this exquisite show every June, held at Rosecliff on Bellevue Avenue. The show includes a judged competitive horticulture display tent and a garden marketplace. Inside the mansion the Rhode Island Federation of Garden Clubs creates beautiful—and I mean beautiful— competitive floral arrangements and displays.

The Rhode Island Spring Flower & Garden Show (401-272-0980; www.flowershow.com). This annual show is held at the Rhode Island Convention Center usually in mid- to late February. It is the first flower show of the year in New England. Always designed on a theme, its display gardens are many and varied; there are education programs, master gardener booths, plant societies and organizations, a marketplace and a landscape design forum. It's a day (or more) well spent.

Garden Clubs and Organizations

American Horticultural Society (www.ahs.org). The grand-daddy of horticultural organizations, the AHS (founded in 1922) is one of the oldest national garden organizations in the country.

The Apeiron Institute for Environmental Living— Sustainable Rhode Island (www.apeiron.org). A Rhode Island organization focused on promoting sustainable living and agriculture, particularly in southeastern New England.

Farm Fresh Rhode Island (www.farmfreshri.org). A nonprofit organization that links Rhode Islanders with local and organic foods, produce, flowers, plants, nurseries, farmers' markets, farm stands, community supported agriculture, and much more.

Gardening for Good (www.gardening4good.org). Founded by Rhode Islander Mary Beth Miller, a horticultural therapist and URI CE Master Gardener, Gardening for Good is a national non-profit organization that reaches out to professionals, individuals, and caregivers with ideas and programs that help older adults continue to enjoy gardening and nature.

New England Carnivorous Plant Society (www.necps.org). Founded by Rhode Islander John Phillip Jr., NECPS is relatively new but very active. It is the only organization in New England dedicated to carnivorous plants.

New England Wild Flower Society (www.newfs.org). One of the most active and substantial plant societies in the country, the New England Wild Flower Society focuses on native plantings and wildflowers and educates about conservation and eradicating invasive plants.

Ocean State Orchid Society (www.oceanstateorchidsociety .org). An affiliate of the American Orchid Society.

Rhode Island American Begonia Society (www.begonia

.org). A fledgling but energetic organization.

Rhode Island Department of Environmental Management, Division of Agriculture (www.rigrown.ri.gov).

Rhode Island Farm Ways (www.rifarm ways.org). This is the Rhode Island Center for Agricultural Promotion & Education (RICAPE), a nonprofit that provides resources to farmers, gardeners, and agricultural professionals to promote sustainable agriculture. The program *A Garden in Every School* is an initiative of RICAPE.

Rhode Island Federation of Garden Clubs (www.garden central.org/rigardenclubs). From Apple Blossom to Wantaknohow, there is a club for you—about thirty-two in all. A marvelous organization that does much more than beautify the neighborhood—community work, education, consulting, floral competitions . . .

Rhode Island Invasive Species Council. See the listing in the "Invasive Plants" section.

Rhode Island Nursery & Landscape Association (www.rinla .org). RINLA is a professional association ready and willing to help home owners, landscapers, arborists, and nursery owners. Make use of them.

Rhode Island Orchid Society (www.riorchidsociety.org). RIOS is a member of the American Orchid Society.

Rhode Island Rose Society. See the listing in the "Annuals and Perennials" section.

Rhode Island Wild Plant Society (www.riwps.org). RIWPS is one of the most productive and energetic organizations for learning about wild plants, invasive plants, natural and native plantings, herbs, and more.

Save the Bay (www.savebay.org). This terrific resource for gardeners offers information about coastal plantings, buffer zones, and other strategies to protect the Narragansett Bay. The brochure *Yard Care Guide for the Coastal Homeowner,* available on the Web site, includes lists of recommended native plants.

Southside Community Land Trust (www.southsideclt.org).

SCLT owns and operates City Farm and Urban Edge (see more in "Public Gardens"). But more than that they are a force in education in Rhode Island, offering many programs, workshops, etc. Get on their e-mail list.

The Urban Environmental Lab Community Garden (401-863-2715). Eighteen individual garden plots grow at the site located at 135 Angell Street, Providence. The UEL was established on the site of a former parking lot. The project was designed to demonstrate how to maximize organic food production in a limited amount of space in an urban environment.

Public Gardens

Blithewold Mansion, Gardens & Arboretum, One Old Ferry Road (Route 114), Bristol 02809; (401) 253-2707; www.blithe wold.org. A forty-five-room mansion on thirty-three acres of historic landscaped gardens, arboretum, woody plants, display gardens, rock garden, water garden, all on the Narragansett Bay. One of only two arboreta in the country on salt water. Open year-round, they offer programs and workshops.

Casey Farm, 2325 Boston Neck Road, Saunderstown 02874; (401) 295-1030; www.historicnewengland.org. A working historic farm with organically grown vegetables, herbs and flowers. Great education programs, a CSA, and a terrific Mother's Day plant sale.

Christopher Arboretum, University of Rhode Island, Kingston 02881; Cooperative Extension: (401) 874-2900. Specimen trees on campuswide self-guided walking tour.

City Farm, corner of Dudley and West Clifford Streets, Providence 02907; (401) 273-9419; www.southsideclt.org. A working model of urban agriculture. Once a neglected vacant lot, this three-quarter-acre certified organic farm demonstrates the productivity of biointensive growing methods for vegetables, herbs, and flowers in an urban location.

Coggeshall Farm Museum, off Poppasquosh Road, Bristol 02809; (401) 253-9062; www.coggeshallfarm.org. A living historical farm museum set on forty acres that has been worked since the seventeenth century. Vegetable and herb gardens, educational programming, and lectures.

East Farm, University of Rhode Island, Route 108, Kingston 02881; (401) 874-2900; www.uri.edu/cels.pls. Research facility and farm operated by the College of the Environment and Life Sciences with display gardens and greenhouses. Of note are the crab apple and rhododendron collections and vegetable selections. Open to the public. Annual spring festival and plant sale.

Gleaner Gardens, 299 Gleaner Chapel Road, North Scituate 02857; (401) 934-9212. Call first to make sure they are open. A private garden now open to the public with more than one hundred varieties of rhododendrons on the property. They also sell some of the plants.

Green Animals Topiary Garden, 380 Corys Lane, Portsmouth 02871; (401) 683-1267; www.newportmansions.org. A small country estate overlooking the Narragansett Bay with lovely display gardens and historic topiary in the shape of animals—some of them very large.

Heber W. Youngken Jr. Medicinal Plant Garden, University of Rhode Island, Kingston 02881; (401) 792-2751; www.uri.edu/pharmacy/garden. Well-labeled medicinal plant garden and greenhouses. Make sure to include it in your visit to the URI Botanical Gardens.

The James Mitchell Varnum House, 57 Pierce Street, East Greenwich 02818; (401) 884-1776; www.varnumcontinentals.org/

house.htm. It is more of a museum, but it has two acres of historic, formal Colonial gardens with views of Greenwich Bay.

Kinney Azalea Gardens, 2391 Kingstown Road (Route 108), Kingston 02881; (401) 783-2396. A spectacular display of more than 800 varieties of azaleas and rhododendrons. Many of the plants are for sale. It does not have a Web site, but if you Google the name you will find a couple of lovely online descriptions with photos.

Linden Place, 500 Hope Street, Bristol 02809; (401) 253-0390; www.lindenplace.org. A small historic garden with many specialty roses in downtown Bristol.

Mount Hope Farm, 250 Metacom Avenue, Bristol 02809; (401) 254-1745; www.mthopefarm.org. Historic landscape saltwater farm from 1745 on 200 acres overlooking the Narragansett Bay. Wildlife trails and gardens. They often host garden events like the Bristol Garden Club Flower Show.

Newport mansions, www.newportmansions.org. Many of the Newport mansions have spectacular gardens and specimen trees. The Web site lists them all: You'll find the Breakers on Ochre Point Avenue, with parterre borders, greenhouses, and gardens; Chateau-sur-Mer on Bellevue Avenue, one of the finest arboretums in Rhode Island; the Elms on Bellevue Avenue, with classical revival gardens and whose historic landscape includes the famous newly restored Sunken Garden. Hunter House at 54 Washington Street features a colonial herb garden, wisteria-covered pergola, perennials, and annuals. Marble House on Bellevue Avenue has formal grounds with mature specimen trees. Rosecliff on Bellevue Avenue offers a historic rose garden, heirloom plant varieties; it's home to the Newport Flower Show.

Prescott Farm, 2009 West Main Road, Middletown 02842; (401) 847-6230; www.newportrestoration.com. Dates from 1730 on thirty-eight acres of farmland; historic landscape and herb gardens. Purchased by Doris Duke in the 1930s. Some of the gardens, particularly the historically accurate herb garden and vegetable garden, are maintained by the URI Cooperative Extension Master Gardeners.

Roger Williams Park Botanical Center, 950 Elmwood Avenue, Providence 02905; (401) 785-9450; www.provi denceri.com/botanical-center. Located in the "Jewel of Providence," Roger Williams Park, this glorious botanical center opened in March 2007. The center encompasses a new conservatory, renovated older greenhouses, and outdoor gardens. It features the largest public indoor display gardens in New England as well as outdoor gardens, and it offers horticultural programming in collaboration with twelve partner groups, including URI Cooperative Extension Master Gardeners, URI College of the Environment and Life Sciences, and the URI Cooperative Extension. There is an orchid garden, cactus garden, water garden, carnivorous plant garden, tropical garden, water features, Asian garden, and more.

Rough Point, Bellevue Avenue, Newport 02840; (401) 849-7300; www.newportrestoration.com. Former estate of Doris Duke. Small historic landscape and gardens overlooking the ocean.

Salve Regina University, 100 Ochre Point Avenue, Newport 02840; (401) 847-6650; www.salve.edu.com. Eighteen historic buildings from Newport's Gilded Age with some formal landscaping and specimen trees on a self-guided campuswide walking garden tour.

More Public Gardens

Each July/August issue of *People, Places & Plants* magazine (www.ppplants .com) lists all of the public gardens in New England, including some thirty in Rhode Island.

Smith's Castle, 55 Richard Smith Drive, Wickford 02852; (401) 294-3521; www.smithscastle.org. A historically accurate herb and flower garden on the water.

Urban Edge, 35 Pippin Orchard Road, Cranston 02921; (401) 273-9419; www.southsideclt.org. Owned and run by Southside Community Land Trust, this fifty-acre farm is being restored to active farmland. Incubator farmers learn to grow, harvest, and market their own produce. If you're interested in vegetable gardening, it's a great visit.

URI Botanical Gardens (formerly the Learning Landscape), University of Rhode Island Cooperative Extension, 3 East Alumni Avenue, Kingston 02881; (401) 874-2900; www.uri.edu/ce/ceec. Designed to showcase sustainable plants and the URI Cooperative Extension Master Gardener Program, these gardens are chock-full of wonderful plants and features, including a beautiful water garden and vegetable garden.

Watson Farm, 455 North Road, Jamestown 02835; (401) 423-0005; www.historicnewengland.org. Two hundred eighty acres of historic working seaside farm. Large vegetable garden with many heirloom vegetables, herbs, compost-making areas, and trails.

Books

The Adventurous Gardener: Where to Buy the Best Plants in New England by Ruah Donnelly

Backyard Giants: The Passionate, Heartbreaking, and Glorious Quest to Grow the Biggest Pumpkin Ever by Susan Warren

Building a Healthy Lawn by Stuart Franklin

Carrots Love Tomatoes by Louis Riotte

Coastal Plants from Cape Cod to Cape Canaveral by Irene H. Stuckey and Lisa Lofland Gould

The Complete Gardener's Almanac: A Month by Month Guide to Successful Gardening by Marjorie Willison

Drought-Tolerant Plants: Waterwise Gardening for Every Climate by Jane Taylor

The Four Season Harvest by Eliot Coleman

A Gardener's Guide to Frost: Outwit the Weather and Extend the Spring and Fall Seasons by Philip Harnden

Garden Insects of North America: The Ultimate Guide to Backyard Bugs by Whitney Cranshaw

The Garden Primer by Barbara Damrosch

A Guide to Rhode Island's Natural Places by Elizabeth Gibbs, Tony Corey, Malia Schwartz, Deborah Grossman-Garber, Carole Jaworski, and Margaret Bucheit

Handbook of Successful Organic Lawn Care by Paul D. Sachs

Insect and Mite Pests of Shade Trees and Woody Ornamentals by Robert Childs and Jennifer Konieczny

Just the Facts! by Garden Way Publishing

The Lawn Bible by David Mellor

Meetings with Remarkable Trees by Thomas Pakenham

Native Trees, Shrubs, and Vines by William Cullina

The Natural Shade Garden by Ken Druse

The New England Gardener's Book of Lists by Karan Davis Cutler

The New York Times 1000 Gardening Questions & Answers

A Northeast Gardener's Year by Lee Reich

The Organic Gardener's Home Reference: A Plant-by-Plant Guide to Growing Fresh, Healthy Food by Tanya Denckla

The Organic Lawn Care Manual by Paul Tukey

Park's Success with Seeds by Anne Reilly

The Perennial Gardener by Frederick McGourty

The Practical Gardener by Roger Swain

The Private Life of Plants by David Attenborough

Reading the Forested Landscape: A Natural History of New England by Tom Wessels

Rhode Island: A History by William G. McLoughlin

Rodale's Illustrated Encyclopedia of Organic Gardening edited by Pauline Pears

The Rose by the American Rose Society

Roses: A Care Manual by Amanda Beales

Roses Love Garlic by Louise Riotte

Seascape Gardening from New England to the Carolinas by Anne Halpin and Roger Foley

Seasons at Sea Meadow: Gardening and other Pleasures on Block Island by Jane Boone Foster

Soils of Rhode Island Landscapes by William R. Wright and Edward H. Sautter

Soil Survey of Rhode Island by Dean D. Rector

Trees of Newport: On the Estates of the Preservation Society of Newport County by Richard L. Champlin

The Vegetable Gardener's Bible by Edward C. Smith

Weeds of the Northeast by Richard H. Uva, Joseph C. Neal, and Joseph M. DiTomaso

Magazines and Radio

EdibleRhody magazine (www.ediblerhody.com). Not a garden magazine as such but, as part of the national magazine family Edible Communities Publications, this quarterly magazine celebrates the foods and traditions of Rhode Island and advocates for organic and locally grown food and produce.

Fine Gardening (www.finegardening.com). An excellent magazine with a section specific to New England. They also publish a selection of books.

Garden Guys radio show (www.garden-guys.com). "Talk Radio Goes Organic"—Sam Jeffries and Fred Jackson air Sunday from 8:00 to 10:00 a.m. on WHJJ 920AM; call (866) 920-9455. Great radio show—the knowledgeable hosts take your questions on air and often have wonderful guests. They sometimes broadcast live from garden events like the Rhode Island Flower Show.

Horticulture (www.hortmag.com). A venerable horticultural

institution; the magazine has a regional section for New England. *Horticulture* also publishes garden books.

People, Places & Plants (www.ppplants.com). A magazine that focuses exclusively on gardening in the Northeast. PPP-TV produces a television show of the same name on HGTV hosted by Roger Swain and Paul Tukey.

The Providential Gardener (www.providentialgardener .typepad.com). Linking Rhode Island's "Growing Community." A terrific source of information for gardeners all over the state, the site is maintained by avid URI CE Master Gardener Susan Korté.

Annuals and Perennials

All-America Rose Selections (www.rose.org). A nonprofit association of rose growers dedicated to the introduction and promotion of exceptional roses.

All-America Selections (www.all-americaselections.org). A nonprofit organization that evaluates plants impartially. AAS celebrated its seventy-fifth anniversary in 2007. URI is working to create a Rhode Island AAS display garden on the university campus.

American Rose Society (www.ars.org). A wealth of information about roses.

Blooms of Bressingham (www.bloomsofbressingham.com). Branded plants from the Bloom family of horticulturists in England.

Perennial Plant Association (www.perennialplant.org). A professional trade association that selects and promotes one perennial plant each year. The association celebrated its twenty-fifth anniversary in 2007.

Perry's Perennial Plants (www.uvm.edu/~pass/perry/). Dr. Leonard Perry, extension professor at the University of Vermont, shares his expertise on this Web site.

Proven Winners (www.provenwinners.com). Branded plants.

Rhode Island Rose Society (www.rirs.org). Affiliated with the American Rose Society and part of the ARS Yankee District.

USDA Plant Database (www.plants.usda.gov). A national database of plant information. You can see a listing of plants in your state, wetlands in the state, endangered plants all over the United States, and noxious and invasive plants, and you can contribute plant information.

Climate, Weather, and Water

Clean Air—Cool Planet and **University of New Hampshire Climate Education Initiative** (www.cleanair-coolplanet.org; www.sustainableunh.unh.edu/climate_ed). Partnered Web sites give data on global warming and show ways you can help stop or slow the trend.

Groundwater Foundation (www.groundwater.org). Educating and motivating people to care for and about groundwater.

Healthy Landscapes (www.uri.edu/ce/healthylandscapes) is a program that comes out of the URI College of the Environment and Life Sciences. Its primary focus is to educate the public about water, water conservation, using water wisely in the landscape, and managing pollution. Jam-packed with great information.

National Arbor Day Foundation Hardiness Zone map (www.arborday.org). Published in 2006, this is the foundation's update of the 1990 USDA Hardiness Zone map. It reflects a warmer climate.

National Atlas of the United States of America (www.nationalatlas.gov). Look under Climate to locate a map of Rhode Island with its precipitation clearly illustrated.

National Drought Mitigation Center (http://drought .unl.edu/dm/monitor). A drought-monitoring site.

National Ground Water Association (www.ngwa.org). Education about groundwater.

National Weather Service (www.nws.noaa.gov).

Rain Barrel Guide (www.rainbarrelguide.com). An excellent guide to rain barrels, with names of suppliers.

Rhode Island Sea Grant College Program (www.seagrant .gso.uri.edu). This federal-state partnership with URI conducts research of particular interest to folks who live and garden near the water—which is pretty much everyone in the Ocean State. RISG publishes *The Water Front,* which highlights the complex interdependence of land and water.

USDA Hardiness Zone map (www.usna.usda.gov/Hardzone/ ushzmap.html). View hardiness zones for any part of the United States in this 1990 map.

U.S. Geological Survey (www.usgs.gov). Compiles water-use estimates for counties in the United States; find details under Drought Watch.

Wunderground (www.wunderground.com). A fun site with lots of climate data.

Invasive Plants

Center for Invasive Plant Management (www.weedcenter.org). A good overview of the national problem, but less focused on the Northeast.

Ecology and Management of Invasive Plants Program (www.invasiveplants.net). Focuses on work conducted by students and staff at Cornell University.

Environment Council of Rhode Island (401-621-8048; www.environmentcouncilri.org). The state affiliate of the National Wildlife Federation.

Invasive Plant Atlas of New England (www.invasives.uconn .edu). Detailed lists of all the invasive plant species.

National Gardening Association (www.garden.org/weed library). Comprehensive list of weeds.

National Invasive Species Information Center (www.invasivespeciesinfo.gov).

Natural Heritage & Endangered Species Program, Rhode Island Division of Fisheries and Wildlife (www.nhesp.org).

New England Wild Flower Society (www.newfs.org). A mecca for any gardener interested in native plants and for those seeking solutions to the problem of invasive plants. The Web site includes the Rhode Island Prohibited Plant List and a list of native substitutes for ornamental invasives.

Rhode Island Biodiversity Center (www.rinhs.org) is a forum to promote the exchange of ideas, news, and questions related to natural history in the state. It offers links to the Rhode Island Invasive Species Council.

Rhode Island Invasive Species Council (www.rinhs.org). This is an outreach of the Rhode Island Natural History Survey, the Rhode Island Agricultural Experiment Station, and URI Cooperative Extension.

Rhode Island Natural History Survey (www.rinhs.org). A consortium of organizations and individuals seeking to advance knowledge and understanding of the Ocean State's biology, geology, and ecosystems. The Web site will link you to the Rhode Island Invasive Species Council and the Rhode Island list of invasives.

Rhode Island Prohibited Plant List. This can be accessed through a number of Web sites, including that of the Rhode Island Wild Plant Society (www.riwps.org) or the Rhode Island Natural History Survey (www.rinhs.org).

United States National Arboretum (www.usna.usda.gov/gardens/invasives.html).

Wild Ones (www.for-wild.org). A nonprofit national educational organization seeking to educate its members and the community about the benefits of using local native plant species in natural landscaping. It does not currently have a chapter in Rhode Island but would like to start one.

Land and Turf Care

Northeast Organic Farming Association of Rhode Island (www.nofari.org). Part of the national association, the Rhode Island chapter is small but evolving. NOFA is a tremendous source of organic information for the home gardener and small farmer. Publications from NOFA/Massachusetts (www.nofama.org) include *A Citizen's Guide to Organic Land Care,* the *Organic Food Guide* and the *NOFA Guide to Organic Land Care: The Directory of Accredited Organic Land Care Professionals in the Northeast.* A handbook on organic lawn and turf care is forthcoming.

SafeLawns (www.safelawns.org). A collaborative effort of garden professionals educating gardeners and home owners about nontoxic lawn care.

Skogley Memorial Turfgrass Research Facility, University of Rhode Island (www.uri.edu/cels/pls/outreachturf.html). Read about the research at one of the oldest turfgrass research centers in the country. And URI's Turfgrass Program offers lots of information: www.uriturf.org.

Toxics Information Project (TIP) (www.toxicsinfo.org). A Rhode Island based organization, TIP publishes the *Less Toxic Landscaping Resource Directory* that lists land-care professionals who use nontoxic methods and products.

Turf Resource Center (www.TurfGrassSod.org). Nonprofit, online source of detailed and general information for both the consumer and the industry.

Landscape Architects or Designers

American Society of Landscape Architects (www.asla.org). Click on Products & Services and type in "Rhode Island" to get a listing of all member landscape architects.

Association of Professional Landscape Designers (www.apld .com; New England region: www.apldne.org). Offers a certification program to encourage professional recognition and standards. Visit the New England site and click on Find a Designer.

Pests and Diseases

Refer also to the "URI Cooperative Extension Master Gardeners" section at the beginning of this chapter.

Massachusetts Introduced Pests Outreach Project (www.mass nrc.org/pests/factsheets.htm). A collaboration between the UMass Extension Agriculture and Landscape Program and the Rhode Island Department of Agricultural Resources. Fact sheets on a huge number of insects, weeds, diseases, and nematodes; links for reporting pest sightings; and other resources.

Northeastern IPM Center (www.NortheastIPM.org). Part of a nationwide system established by the USDA to provide information about integrated pest management across the Northeast.

Pro New England (www.pronewengland.org) is an online resource and directory.

Soil

Coastal Zone Soil Survey Initiative (www.MapCoast.org). In 2004 the Mapping Partnership for Coastal Soil and Sediment was formed to facilitate the collection of more detailed soil and sediment data for coastal marshes, shallow water habitats, dunes, and intertidal flats. In 2007, as part of the Coastal Zone Soil Survey, the Rhode Island Natural Resources Conservation Service established a center for coastal soil mapping.

Composters.com (www.composters.com). An online source of worm bins and "worm accessories." Find additional composting Web sites by searching "purchasing worm bins" online. And see the later entry for the Worm Ladies of Charlestown.

Laboratory of Soil Ecology and Microbiology (www.uri .edu/cels/nrs/seml/index.html). Two faculty members from the

Department of Natural Resources at the University of Rhode Island, Josef Görres and Jose Amador, are collaborating to understand the "interplay among microorganisms, fauna and plants, the biogeochemical processes they carry out, and the physical environment in which their activities take place."

Office of the Rhode Island State Soil Scientist (401-822-8830; www.ri .nrcs.usda.gov/technical/soils.html or www.nesoil.com). Excellent USDA Web site with in-depth information on soils and weather. Research the soil surveys for your county's soil from this site. Also sells the manuals *Soils of Rhode Island Landscapes* by William R. Wright and Edward H. Sautter and the *Soil Survey of Rhode Island* by Dean D. Rector of the Soil Conservation Service. Or you can write to the local office: Office of the State Soil Scientist, USDA Natural Resources Conservation Service, 60 Quaker Lane, Suite 46, Warwick 02886.

Rhode Island Resource Conservation & Development Area Council (401-826-2409; www.rircd.org). Contact the council to find DEM-certified composting facilities.

Rhode Island Resource Recovery (401-942-1430; www.rirrc.org). A state environmental agency that provides the public with environmentally sound programs and facilities to manage solid waste. Good information on composting.

Soil Science Society of America (www.soils.org). Lists good publications about soils and crops.

Worm Ladies of Charlestown (www.angoraandworms.com). Lois Fulton and Nancy Warner raise and sell worms (red wigglers) for composting. They give workshops on the process of making worm compost, otherwise known as vermiculture.

Soil Tests

University of Massachusetts Extension Service (www.umass .edu/plsoils/soiltest). The University of Rhode Island no longer performs soil tests for home owners, so the closest place is UMass Amherst, where they offer a variety of soil and compost tests for a relatively small fee. Get details online or write to the Soil and Plant Tissue Testing Laboratory, West Experiment Station, 682 North Pleasant Street, University of Massachusetts, Amherst, MA 01003. UMass Amherst soil sample kits are often sold in local garden centers.

URI Cooperative Extension Master Gardener Program (401-874-2900; www.urimga.org) will also provide information on where to find soil test kits in Rhode Island.

Trees and Shrubs

Cary Award (www.caryaward.org). Promotes outstanding plants for New England gardens based at Tower Hill Botanic Garden in Boylston, Massachusetts.

National Arbor Day Foundation (www.arborday.org/treeinfo/ treehealth.cfm). Offers links to certified arborists and features the Arbor Day hardiness zone map.

Rhode Island Arborists (www.rinla.org). You can easily find a certified arborist from the Rhode Island Nursery & Landscape Association Web site.

Rhode Island Department of Environmental Management's Division of Forest Environment (www.dem.ri.gov/program) has a program called Rhode Island Tree Stewardship and publishes a downloadable publication *Forest Stewardship* about the state's forests and trees.

Rhode Island Tree Council (www.ritree.org). A fabulous organization dedicated to educating the public to increase awareness of the value of trees. Offers educational programming and tree stewardship training.

Tree Care Industry Association (www.tcia.org). Accredits tree care companies and establishes standards of tree care practice. Visit the Web site and enter your zip code to find a certified arborist in your area.

University of Rhode Island Cooperative Extension and Department of Plant Sciences and Entomology (www.uri.edu/research/sustland). Offers an online list of sustainable trees and shrubs for New England.

Vegetables

Community Supported Agriculture farms and farmers' markets can be found on two good Web sites in the state. Learn more about CSAs and locate local farms that will sell you vegetables through this program. Find farmers' markets and wineries around the state, a calendar of events, a complete list of Rhode Island-grown products and an agriculture tourism map. Visit Farm Fresh Rhode Island (www.farmfreshri.org) and the RI Department of Environmental Management's Rhode Island Grown (www.dem.ri.gov).

Southern New England Giant Pumpkins Growers Association (401-864-7747). Tips for growing competition-sized pumpkins.

University of Massachusetts Extension (www.umassvegetable .org; www.nevegetable.org). Features *The New England Vegetable*

Management Guide, a collaborative effort with members of the extension vegetable programs of the Universities of Maine, New Hampshire, Vermont, Connecticut, and Rhode Island.

Wildlife

Audubon Society of Rhode Island (401 949-5788; www.asri .org). Information about wildlife and encouraging wildlife in your garden, plus a list of wildlife refuges. Beautiful education center in Bristol offers a boardwalk out into the salt marshes and a good shop.

Glossary

acid soil: Soil with a pH lower than 7.

alkaline soil: Soil with a pH higher than 7.

annual: A plant that germinates, grows to maturity, sets seed, and dies all in one growing season.

antitranspirant: A solution sprayed on plants to decrease water loss through foliage.

bacteria: Organisms that cause disease.

balled and burlapped: A tree or shrub dug from the ground with a ball of soil around the roots that has been wrapped in burlap or similar material.

bare root: A plant with no soil or very little soil around the roots.

beneficials: A term used to identify those insects that benefit the gardener.

biennial: A plant that germinates, grows to maturity, sets seed, and dies over a two-year period.

botanical controls: Products derived from naturally occurring sources that are used to eradicate weeds and other noxious plants.

branch collar: The area at the base of a branch where it meets the trunk.

caliper: A measurement of the diameter of a tree's trunk.

clay soils: Soils predominantly made of tiny mineral particles.

climate: Weather conditions that happen in a specific region.

cold frame: A box, with a see-through lid, that is set in the ground and into which plants are either sown or set in pots to protect them against the cold.

companion planting: A planting technique in which plants that are thought to protect or benefit each other are grown together.

compost: A product of decomposed organic matter, usually made of a balance of "brown" and "green" plant material.

compost tea: A brew made by steeping compost in water; used as a foliar spray or liquid fertilizer.

container grown: Referring to a plant that was started in and grown on in a container.

cool-weather crops: Plants that do not tolerate heat and are therefore more likely to be early spring or fall crops.

corn gluten meal: A product used to eliminate weeds; it works by stopping a germinating plant's root formation.

cover crops: Plants that are grown for a season and then tilled into the soil, thus putting organic matter back into the soil. Also known as green manure.

crop rotation: A planting technique that ensures plants from the same botanical family are not grown in the same spot every year.

damping-off: A fungal disease that is often a problem during seed germination.

deadheading: Pinching or cutting spent blooms to stimulate the plant into putting energy into new blooms.

diatomaceous earth: Crushed fossilized skeletons of marine creatures used to control some insects.

disease triangle: An approach to understanding how plant disease develops; states that three factors must be present, a susceptible plant, a pathogen, and the right environmental conditions.

drip irrigation: A method of watering that uses hoses with tiny outlets called emitters that dispense water directly to the soil at targeted spots.

field grown: Referring to plants that are started in the field and later dug up and grown in a container.

fungal diseases: Diseases caused by fungus; rot, decay, and mold are indicators of fungal disease.

glacial till: A mix of sand, silt, and clay that resulted from glacier action.

growing season: The number of days between the last frost of the spring and the first of the fall.

grub: Larva stage of an insect during its life cycle.

half-hardy annuals: Annual plants that can handle a slight frost.

half-hardy perennials: Plants need some protection (such as mulch) from winter cold.

hardening off: The process of acclimatizing plants grown indoors to outdoor temperatures.

hardiness zone: Usually refers to a USDA Hardiness Zone designation, one of 11 areas, or zones, each based on a 10-degree Fahrenheit difference in average annual minimum temperatures. Plant hardiness zones are used to help identify which plants will survive low temperatures.

hardy annuals: Annuals that can be sown outdoors in spring, before the last frost, as soon as the ground can be worked. Some can be sown in the fall for spring germination.

hardy perennials: Plants that can survive very cold winters without protection or with very little protection.

herbaceous perennial: A plant with stems, leaves, and flowers that die back to the ground in fall and regrow in spring.

herbicide: A substance that kills plants.

hoop house: A hooped structure for protecting plants; can be as large as a greenhouse or small and movable.

horticultural oil: A substance that is sprayed on plants to suffocate insects.

insecticidal soap: A substance made from potassium salts of fatty acids used to control or kill insects.

insecticide: A substance that kills insects.

integrated pest management (IPM): A commonsense, ecologically friendly method of dealing with the problems of disease and pest damage, with an emphasis on using the least toxic approach.

interplanting: Growing two or more crops together in the same place to their mutual benefit.

invasive plants: Plants not native to the United States that crowd out native species and cause environmental and economic harm.

irrigation zones: An area where plants with similar water needs are grown together.

leader: A main tree stem or trunk.

leaf scar: The mark left on a branch when a leaf falls off.

lime: Calcium carbonate; used to raise the soil pH level.

loam: A balanced mix of sand, silt, and clay with good texture, good drainage, and the right amounts of moisture and air.

manure: Animal droppings often used as a soil amendment.

microbial activity: The activity of microbes in the soil.

microclimate: Pockets of warmer or colder temperatures within a hardiness zone.

milky disease: A bacteria (*Bacillus popillae*) that attacks some, but not all, grubs in the soil.

mulch: Compost, wood chips, buckwheat hulls, or other materials applied on top of soil to help conserve water and keep weeds down.

Narragansett Silt Loam: The unofficial state soil of Rhode Island, named after the area known as Narragansett.

native plant: A plant that has been growing in North America since before European settlement.

neem: An organic insecticide derived from the neem tree; it interrupts hormonal activity.

nematodes: Microscopic worms that attack insects.

neutral soil: Soil with a pH of 7.0, which is midway between acid and alkaline.

nutrients: The elements needed by a plant for healthy growth.

organic matter: Material made by plants and animals.

parasitoid: Referring to insect parasites that live on or in a host insect.

parent material: The third soil layer, or horizon, which roots cannot penetrate.

perennial: A plant that comes back and lives year after year.

pH: A measurement of how alkaline or acid the soil. The measurements range from 1 to 14, with 1 to 5 acidic, 8 to 14 alkaline, and 6 to 7 considered neutral.

pheromone traps: Devices filled with insect hormones and used to trap insects.

pollinator: An insect that transfers pollen from the anther to the stigma in a flower.

predators: Insects that attack other insects.

rain barrel: A container to catch rainwater, usually placed at the bottom of a downspout.

red wiggler: An earthworm—either *Eisenia fetida* or *Lumbricus rubellus*—used in making compost. *See* vermiculture.

rhizomes: Stems that travel under the surface of the soil.

sandy soils: Soils predominantly made of large mineral particles.

self-sowers: Annuals or biennials that deposit their seeds in the garden and the seeds germinate the following year.

silty soils: Soils made predominantly of medium-size mineral particles.

soaker hose: An irrigation hose that "sweats" water along its entire length.

sod: Fully grown turf that is cut in strips ready to be laid in a prepared bed to create an instant lawn.

soil amendments: Materials added to the soil to improve it, such as animal manure, slow-release organic fertilizers, cover crops, and compost.

soil color: An indication of how much organic material that soil contains. The darker the color the greater the organic matter content.

soil fertility: A reference to how rich the soil is in nutrients and organic matter.

soil horizon: One of three layers of soil; the soil horizons are topsoil, subsoil, and parent material.

soil structure: The soil's physical condition.

soil test: An analysis of a soil's pH, nutrient content, texture, and other factors.

soil texture: Refers to how much clay, silt, or sand is in the soil.

stolons: Stems that travel just above the surface of the soil.

subshrub: *See* woody perennial.

subsoil: The second layer, or horizon, of soil. There's less root growth in this layer.

succession planting: Growing one crop after another so that the garden is in use for the entire growing season. Often used in vegetable gardening.

surface horizon: *See* topsoil.

synthetic fertilizer: Manmade, nonorganic fertilizer.

tender annuals: Annuals that don't tolerate the cold and will be killed by frost.

tender perennials: Perennials that won't survive the winter in certain climates and that need to be lifted and stored in cold weather to be replanted in the spring.

thatch: A buildup of organic matter comprising dead and dying stems and roots that settles on the soil surface and interferes with the growth of turfgrass.

thinning: A pruning term that refers to taking entire limbs out from the bottom or back to the trunk.

till: Soil that is a mix of sand, silt, and clay.

tillers: New shoots that form at the base of a plant near the soil.

tilth: *See* soil structure.

topping: A pruning term that refers to the removal of part of a limb probably closer to the end of the limb. Also known as *heading*. An alternative definition of topping means the removal of the entire top of a tree.

topsoil: The first layer or surface horizon of soil; it is usually darker because of the organic content. It is in this layer that most of the root action takes place so plants obtain most of their water and nutrients from this surface horizon.

trunk flare: The area where a tree's roots meet the trunk. Also called the root collar or root flare.

vermicompost: The end-product of worm composting.

vermiculture: Composting with worms.

viral disease: Disease caused by a virus. The entire plant may be stunted in growth and misshapen with yellowing leaves that are mottled and curling with no visible veins.

warm-weather crops: Crops that grow better in warmer temperatures and so are planted later in the season.

woody perennial (woodies): A plant with woody, stiff stems that does not die back to its crown or roots. Often referred to as a subshrub.

xeriscaping: A term for landscaping that uses indigenous and drought-tolerant plants.

Index